maths

6

Extension *for all* through problem solving

Teacher's Handbook

Year 6 / Primary 7

Paul Harrison

Ann Montague-Smith

CAMBRIDGE
UNIVERSITY PRESS
York St John

CAMBRIDGE UNIVERSITY PRESS

Cambridge, New York, Melbourne, Madrid, Cape Town, Singapore,
São Paulo, Delhi, Dubai, Tokyo, Mexico City

Cambridge University Press
The Edinburgh Building, Cambridge CB2 8RU, UK

www.cambridge.org
Information on this title: www.cambridge.org/9780521754972

First published 2003
4th printing 2010

Printed in the United Kingdom by Short Run Press, Exeter

A catalogue record for this publication is available from the British Library

ISBN 978-0-521-75497-2 Paperback

Authors Paul Harrison, Ann Montague-Smith

ACKNOWLEDGEMENTS

Content editing by Pete Crawford

Cover design by Karen Thomas

Text illustration by Liz Pichon

Project management by Cambridge Publishing Management Limited

The authors and publishers would like to thank schools and individuals who trialled lessons.

Contents

Introduction

Lesson plans

3

Introduction

About Apex Maths

Apex Maths uses problem solving to address the needs of the more able and also provides extension and enrichment opportunities for children of all abilities. This allows Apex Maths to be used within the context of the whole-class daily mathematics lesson, reflecting the philosophy of The National Numeracy Strategy *Framework for teaching mathematics*.

Thirty detailed lesson plans are presented in the Teacher's Handbook. Each focuses on a core problem or investigation that is differentiated in various ways so that children of all abilities can work at their own level on the same basic problem.

The lessons address all the problem solving objectives in the *Framework* and span all the other *Framework* strands.

The problems are richer and deeper than the relatively straightforward word problems suggested in the *Framework*, thereby helping to develop thinking skills. They provide contexts in which children can apply and extend their mathematical skills and understanding, and consolidate their problem solving skills.

The teaching approach adopted throughout allows children to use enquiry, creative thinking and reasoning skills to solve a problem, with input from the teacher in the form of probing questions and occasional suggestions and hints. A carefully designed plenary encourages children to discuss their reasoning and evaluate the strategies used.

Teacher's materials

The Teacher's Handbook includes:

Scope and sequence chart
This lists all the problems together with the problem solving objectives addressed (from the *Framework for teaching mathematics*), the likely outcome levels for each ability group for Attainment Target 1 (Using and applying mathematics) in *The National Curriculum for England: mathematics* and the *Framework* topics addressed by each problem.

Scotland 5–14 Guidelines
A chart linking each lesson to related strands in *Curriculum and Assessment in Scotland, National Guidelines: Mathematics 5–14*.

Northern Ireland Lines of Development
A table linking each lesson to related *Northern Ireland Lines of Development* (levels 4 and 5).

Oral and mental problem solving starters
A bank of oral and mental starters with a problem solving slant, which can be used at the start of any lesson.

Lesson plans
These are presented in double-page spreads. A blueprint on pages 8–9 explains the features of the plans. The lesson plans feature different types of problems, including:

- investigations requiring the identification of patterns and the making of generalisations;
- number puzzles and investigations which require reasoning about numbers;
- complex 'real-life' multi-stage problems involving a range of mathematics;
- word problems that are essentially algebraic, where combinations of known values are used to find unknown values.

Useful mathematical information
This is a bank of additional mathematical information, perhaps explaining a particular concept or looking at a particular problem in greater depth.

Pupils' materials

Problems are presented for children in the Pupil's Textbook and/or using Photocopy Masters (PCMs) from the Teacher's Handbook. Sometimes differentiation of a problem involves giving clues or additional direction to the Average or Less able groups. Presenting a problem in two formats helps to avoid children using clues and directions intended for other ability groups.

Where parts of the page are numbered in the Textbook, this generally indicates a progression in the complexity of the problem. The Differentiation section in the Lesson plans indicates which parts of the pupil material are intended for which ability group.

Plenary

The main whole-class interactive teaching part of the lesson, with suggestions for discussion of solutions to the problem, the methods used, problem solving skills and the mathematics involved.

Plenary

Display an enlarged version of Fractions challenge 2.

1 Explain to children that you are going to focus on problem 2, but that the other problems can be dealt with in a similar way. Invite children to explain how the problem can be solved, encouraging children from all groups to contribute. Make sure that the methods are understood. These are likely to be along the following lines.

- Write an expression to find the total of the fractions received by Mindy, Mandy and Mog:
  $\frac{1}{4} + \frac{1}{6} + \frac{1}{12}$

- Use equivalent fractions to express the statement with common denominators and add them up:
  $\frac{1}{4} + \frac{1}{6} + \frac{1}{12} = \frac{3}{12} + \frac{2}{12} + \frac{1}{12} = \frac{6}{12}$ (or $\frac{1}{2}$)

- Work out the fraction that was received by Meg:
  $\frac{12}{12} - \frac{6}{12} = \frac{6}{12}$ (or $\frac{1}{2}$)

- Equate Meg's fraction with the number of coins she got:
  $\frac{6}{12} = 6$ coins. So $\frac{1}{12} = 1$ coin

- Calculate Mog's amount:
  Mog received $\frac{1}{12} = 1$ coin

2 *How can we check the answer?* Discuss and use the children's suggestions. A likely suggestion is as follows:

- Work out how many coins the other children received, knowing that $\frac{1}{12} = 1$ coin.

- Find the total number of coins by adding.

- Work through the problem again, knowing the total number of coins.

3 Establish the correct answers for each of the other problems.

4 Discuss any difficulties that children had with the mathematics involved. These might include:

- Adding fractions.
  Establish that fractions need to be converted to equivalent fractions with the same denominator before they can be added. For fractions such as $\frac{1}{4}$, $\frac{1}{6}$ and $\frac{1}{12}$ (Fractions challenge 2), a fraction wall could be used to change the fractions to twelfths:

1 whole											
$\frac{1}{4}$			$\frac{1}{4}$			$\frac{1}{4}$			$\frac{1}{4}$		
$\frac{1}{6}$		$\frac{1}{6}$		$\frac{1}{6}$		$\frac{1}{6}$		$\frac{1}{6}$		$\frac{1}{6}$	
$\frac{1}{12}$	$\frac{1}{12}$	$\frac{1}{12}$	$\frac{1}{12}$	$\frac{1}{12}$	$\frac{1}{12}$	$\frac{1}{12}$	$\frac{1}{12}$	$\frac{1}{12}$	$\frac{1}{12}$	$\frac{1}{12}$	$\frac{1}{12}$

For sets of fractions such as $\frac{1}{3}$, $\frac{1}{4}$ and $\frac{1}{5}$ (Fractions challenge 3), the lowest common multiple of all the denominators needs to be found. (For a full explanation, see **Useful mathematical information pages 83–84**.)

- Finding the fraction that the last child (Seth, Meg or Jo) received.
  Help children to understand that the whole pot is 1 and that 1 can be represented by any fraction in which the numerator and denominator are the same, for example, $\frac{2}{3}$, $\frac{4}{4}$, $\frac{5}{5}$, $\frac{20}{20}$. So if $\frac{1}{3}$ of the pot is used then the fraction of the pot remaining is $\frac{3}{3} - \frac{1}{3} = \frac{2}{3}$

Development

Children make up similar problems at their level – perhaps using only 2 fractions. They must be able to work out the solution themselves.

Solutions

Fractions challenge 1
Jill got 2 coins.

Fractions challenge 2
Mog got 1 coin.

Fractions challenge 3
Sandy got 15 coins.

41

Useful mathematical information reference

A reference to indicate where you can find additional information about the mathematics involved in a problem.

Development

Ideas for children to develop the problem, perhaps at home. They can also be used for children who manage to complete a problem early on in the lesson.

Solutions

Solutions to the problem at all levels for quick reference.

9

Lesson structure

Lessons have the recommended 3-part structure, but there is a slightly different emphasis on each part. As it is intended that children solve the problem in their own way, your input at the start of the activity is comparatively brief and is mainly concerned with introducing the problem and checking that children understand what is required.

The main teaching will take place indirectly, through probing questions, hints and suggestions as children work. Direct teaching takes place in the plenary, as solutions, problem solving methods and the mathematics involved are discussed. The plenary therefore contains much greater detail than the problem introduction. It offers opportunities for children to:

- use appropriate vocabulary;
- compare their strategies and solutions;
- listen to explanations and develop their understanding of mathematical ideas and strategies;
- ask and answer questions.

Differentiation

The problems in this book are differentiated in various ways:

- By level of difficulty
  Here there are different activities for different ability groups. Early finishers may be able to progress to an activity for a higher ability group.

- By outcome
  Here children are expected to approach the problem in more or less sophisticated ways, applying mathematical knowledge and understanding at their own level.

- By resource used as support
  Here children can choose different resources to support them, such as working mentally, using pencil and paper, using an empty number line or using a 100 square. Sometimes a hint may be provided for lower ability groups.

- By level of support
  Here, especially where additional adults are available, groups can be targeted for specific support.

Questioning techniques

There will be many opportunities to ask questions during a problem solving lesson.

Closed questions will give a response of yes or no, or will elicit specific knowledge. They can be used to check understanding. Examples include:

- *Do you understand?* (yes/no)
- *What is half of three hundred?* (one hundred and fifty)

Open questions allow children the opportunity to give a range of responses. Examples include:

- *What fractions of what numbers can you think of that would give the answer of 60?* ($\frac{1}{2}$ of 120; $\frac{1}{4}$ of 240; $\frac{3}{4}$ of 80; $\frac{6}{10}$ of 100 . . .)
- *How could you solve this problem?*

Probing questions are nearly always open in the sense that they require a carefully thought out answer, through which children explain their mathematics. These questions will give you the opportunity to assess their understanding. Examples include:

- *How did you work that out? Is there another way?*
- *What would happen if the numbers were changed to . . . ? Would that make a difference? Why is that?*
- *Roughly what answer do you expect to get? How did you come to that estimate?*

Optional adult input

Children may need support and encouragement while they gain familiarity and confidence in working in a new way, or if they have limited experience of solving problems. You may find it helpful, if possible, to arrange for some additional classroom help, particularly when first using this resource.

There are suggestions in each lesson plan as to which group any additional adult could help with and in what way. Here are some general suggestions about how to make best use of an additional adult:

- fully brief them about the problem for that lesson and what your expectations are for each ability group;
- make sure that they understand that children should be allowed to solve a problem in their own way, even if at times it appears that they are going down a blind alley;
- encourage use of suggested probing questions from the **Teacher focus for activity** section of each lesson. Also suggest the following 'catch all' questions:
  - *Can you explain what you have done so far?*
  - *Why did you do that?*
  - *What are you going to do next?*

Class organisation

The lessons in Apex Maths have been specifically designed as whole-class numeracy lessons.

The differentiated ways in which the problems are presented make them ideal for mixed age classes. They are also highly suitable for schools where children are grouped according to ability for mathematics lessons. The higher ability sets can work on the main problem and the average and lower ability sets can work on the differentiated presentations of the problem.

In mixed ability classes, children should be broadly grouped in the classroom according to ability. This will facilitate group discussion with the teacher if needed. It will also avoid children 'borrowing' clues or additional directions provided for children of a lesser ability.

Children should ideally work in pairs or threes when they are working on a problem or investigation. This will stimulate discussion – an essential component of the problem solving process.

Resources

Simple resources will be needed to support these activities, all of which are readily available. Some may be essential to the successful outcome of the activity. Others should be made available, so children can make decisions on resources needed.

General resources that may be useful, include:
> digit cards;
> individual whiteboards;
> number lines;
> 100 squares (PCM 9);
> multiplication squares (PCM 9);
> counters and centimetre cubes;
> squared and dotty paper (centimetre squares);
> calculators;
> pin boards (geoboards) and elastic bands.

Calculators

Some problem solving or investigatory procedures might involve many tedious or repetitive calculations that do not develop children's mathematical understanding. Others might involve calculations that are just beyond the ability of children who are otherwise making excellent progress towards solving the problem. In these cases teachers should use their discretion as to whether to allow some children to use a calculator. In lessons in which this situation is likely to occur, 'calculators (discretionary)' is listed with the resources to be made available.

Assessment

While children are working at the problem and during the plenary, target pairs and individuals in order to assess their skills in problem solving. Use probing questions, such as the examples given under **Questioning techniques**, and those given within the teacher's notes for the lesson. By targeting specific children during each problem solving lesson, it is possible to ensure that all children will be assessed through discussion over time.

Look for signs of consistency in approach to a given problem. Make sure that children read all of the data and are able to decide which data is relevant and which should be discarded.

When discussing their work, take the opportunity to identify whether children have understood the mathematics involved. This is an ideal time to check whether there are any misconceptions that need remedying.

Watch for children who rely too heavily upon their partner for:

- how to solve the problem
  Does the child understand what the problem involves?
- mathematical calculations
  Does the child understand which calculation strategies and procedures to use, and can they use these themselves?
- recording the problem
  Is the child able to suggest how the results might be presented?
- answering open and probing questions and reporting back in the plenary
  Is the child able to articulate their thinking? Does the child have the appropriate vocabulary and can they use it appropriately to express mathematical ideas and explanations? Are they given enough response time?

During the problem solving lesson, take time to stand back and observe what the children are doing:

- Do children cooperate?
- Are they working collaboratively?
- Do both partners contribute to the discussion, or does one dominate by taking the lead?
- Do they use appropriate mathematical language in order to express their ideas?

Scope and sequence chart

This lists all the problems together with:

- the problem solving objectives addressed (from the NNS *Framework for teaching mathematics*);
- the likely outcome levels for each ability group for Attainment Target 1 (Using and applying maths) in *The National Curriculum for England: mathematics*;
- the *Framework* topics addressed by each problem.

Because children will solve problems in different ways, using different aspects of mathematics, the specific *Framework* objectives that will be addressed will vary. For this reason, only the topics that are likely to be addressed have been referenced.

* indicates that the general mathematical content may extend the most able beyond the Year 6 objectives in the *Framework for teaching mathematics*

Problem	Problem solving objectives involved						Ma1 Using and applying mathematics Level/Outcome			Mathematical topics
	Choose and use appropriate number operations and ways of calculating . . .	Explain methods and reasoning, orally and in writing.	Solve mathematical problems or puzzles, recognise and explain patterns . . .	Make and investigate a general statement about familiar numbers or shapes . . .	Develop from explaining a generalised relationship in words to expressing it in a formula . . .	Identify and use appropriate operations . . . to solve word problems . . . Explain methods and reasoning	More able	Average	Less able	
1 Cycle tour*	■		■			■	Level 5	Level 5	Level 4	Properties of numbers and number sequences Mental calculation strategies (+, − and ÷) Handling data
2 Queue jumping*		■	■		■		Level 5	Level 4	Level 3	Properties of numbers and number sequences
3 Dartboards	■	■	■				Level 5	Level 5	Level 3	Properties of numbers and number sequences Mental calculation strategies (+ and −)
4 Magic squares		■	■				Level 5	Level 4/5	Level 3	Mental calculation strategies (+ and −)
5 Multiplication investigation		■	■				Level 5	Level 4	Level 3/4	Mental calculation strategies (+ and ×) Understanding × Rapid recall of × facts
6 Financial fudge*	■					■	Level 5	Level 4/5	Level 3	Fractions, decimals, percentages, ratio and proportion Mental calculation strategies (+, −, ×, ÷) Pencil and paper procedures (+, −, ×, ÷) Understanding × and ÷ Checking results of calculations
7 Marco's pizzeria	■					■	Level 5/6	Level 5/6	Level 4	Fractions, decimals, percentages and proportion Mental calculation strategies (+, −, ×, ÷) Understanding × and ÷
8 Make a century!	■		■				Level 5/6	Level 5	Level 4	Mental calculation strategies (+, −, ×, ÷) Understanding × and ÷ Rapid recall of × and ÷ facts Using a calculator

Problem	Problem solving objectives involved						Ma1 Using and applying mathematics Level/Outcome More able	Average	Less able	Mathematical topics
9 Dotty polygons*		■	■	■	■		Level 5/6	Level 4	Level 3	Properties of numbers and number sequences Measures
10 Fractions challenge*	■	■					Level 5	Level 4	Level 3	Fractions, decimals, percentages, ratio and proportion
11 Stamps		■	■			■	Level 5/6	Level 5	Level 4	Properties of numbers and number sequences Mental calculation strategies (+ and ×)
12 Problems at work	■					■	Level 5	Level 4	Level 3/4	Mental calculation strategies (+, − and ×) Checking results of calculations Measures
13 How old?*	■					■	Level 5/6	Level 4/5	Level 3/4	Mental calculation strategies (+ and ×) Pencil and paper procedures (+ and ×) Measures
14 Personal weights	■		■			■	Level 5/6	Level 5	Level 4	Mental calculation strategies (+ and −)
15 Road signs*		■	■	■			Level 5/6	Level 4/5	Level 3/4	Properties of numbers and number sequences Shape and space
16 Calculation investigation*		■	■	■	■		Level 5	Level 4/5	Level 3/4	Place value, ordering and rounding Pencil and paper procedures (+, −, ×, ÷) Rapid recall of × and ÷ facts
17 School disco	■					■	Level 5	Level 4/5	Level 4	Fractions, decimals, percentages, ratio and proportion
18 Window investigations			■	■			Level 5	Level 4/5	Level 3/4	Properties of numbers and number sequences Mental calculation strategies (+, −, ×, ÷)
19 Big time*	■					■	Level 5/6	Level 4/5	Level 4	Mental calculation strategies (+, −, ×, ÷) Pencil and paper procedures (+, −, ×, ÷) Measures
20 Patio patterns*		■	■	■	■		Level 5/6	Level 4	Level 3/4	Properties of numbers and number sequences
21 Broken calculators	■		■				Level 5	Level 4/5	Level 3/4	Fractions, decimals, percentages, ratio and proportion Mental calculation strategies (+, −, ×, ÷) Rapid recall of × and ÷ facts

Problem	Problem solving objectives involved						Ma1 Using and applying mathematics Level/Outcome			Mathematical topics
							More able	Average	Less able	
22 Bargain trainers	■					■	Level 5/6	Level 4/5	Level 3/4	Fractions, decimals, percentages, ratio and proportion Mental calculation strategies (+, −, ×, ÷)
23 Fields and rectangles*		■	■				Level 5	Level 4/5	Level 3	Fractions, decimals, percentages, ratio and proportion Properties of numbers and number sequences Rapid recall of × and ÷ facts Mental calculation strategies (×) Measures
24 Handshakes*		■	■	■	■		Level 5/6	Level 4/5	Level 3/4	Properties of numbers and number sequences
25 Average scores*	■		■		■		Level 5	Level 4/5	Level 4	Mental calculation strategies (+ and −) Rapid recall of × and ÷ facts Handling data
26 Cuboid frames		■	■				Level 5	Level 4/5	Level 4	Properties of numbers and number sequences Measures Shape and space
27 Grid squares		■	■	■	■		Level 5/6	Level 3/4	Level 3/4	Properties of numbers and number sequences Shape and space
28 Economical boxes*		■	■				Level 6	Level 4/5	Level 3/4	Properties of numbers and number sequences Measures Shape and space
29 Investigating diagonals*		■	■	■	■		Level 5/6	Level 4/5	Level 3/4	Properties of numbers and number sequences Shape and space
30 Magic shapes			■				Level 4/5	Level 4/5	Level 3/4	Mental calculation strategies (+ and −)

Scotland 5–14 Guidelines

	Problem solving and enquiry	Information handling	Range and type of numbers	Money	Add and subtract	Multiply and divide	Fractions, percentages and ratio	Patterns and sequences	Functions and equations	Measure and estimate	Time	Perimeter, formulae and scales	Shape, position and movement
1 Cycle tour	•	•			•	•		•		•			
2 Queue jumping	•							•	•				
3 Dartboards	•				•			•					
4 Magic squares	•				•								
5 Multiplication investigation	•				•	•							
6 Financial fudge	•		•	•	•	•							
7 Marco's pizzeria	•		•	•	•	•							
8 Make a century!	•				•	•							
9 Dotty polygons	•							•	•			•	
10 Fractions challenge	•		•				•						
11 Stamps	•		•	•	•			•					
12 Problems at work	•			•	•	•					•		
13 How old?	•		•		•	•					•		
14 Personal weights	•				•					•			
15 Road signs	•							•	•				
16 Calculation investigation	•				•	•			•				
17 School disco	•					•	•						
18 Window investigations	•				•	•		•					
19 Big time	•		•		•	•					•		
20 Patio patterns	•							•	•				
21 Broken calculators	•		•		•	•							
22 Bargain trainers	•		•	•	•	•	•						
23 Fields and rectangles	•					•	•	•		•		•	
24 Handshakes	•							•	•				
25 Average scores	•	•			•	•							
26 Cuboid frames	•							•					•
27 Grid squares	•							•					•
28 Economical boxes	•							•				•	•
29 Investigating diagonals	•							•	•				•
30 Magic shapes	•				•								

In each activity, children will need to employ the three problem-solving steps of (1) starting, (2) doing and (3) reporting on a task. Encourage children to choose appropriate strategies at each stage, and to evaluate their choices.

Northern Ireland Lines of Development (Levels 4 and 5)

'Processes in mathematics' applies to all lessons.

Lesson		Related Lines of Development
1	Cycle tour	M5.1, M5.3, R5.5, HD5.4
2	Queue jumping	R4.3, R5.2, R5.8
3	Dartboards	N4.3, R5.7
4	Magic squares	N4.3, R5.7
5	Multiplication investigation	N4.3, N4.5, R5.7
6	Financial fudge	N4.17, N4.18
7	Marco's pizzeria	N4.17, N4.18
8	Make a century!	N4.3, N4.5, N4.12, R5.6
9	Dotty polygons	M4.8, A4.1, A5.2, R5.8
10	Fractions challenge	N5.6
11	Stamps	N4.3, R4.3
12	Problems at work	T5.3, N4.18
13	How old?	T5.2, N4.14, N5.1
14	Personal weights	M5.3, N4.3, R4.1
15	Road signs	R4.3, R5.2, R5.8
16	Calculation investigation	N5.7, R5.9
17	School disco	N5.10
18	Window investigations	R4.5
19	Big time	T5.2, N5.4
20	Patio patterns	R4.3, R5.8
21	Broken calculators	N4.17, N5.7, N5.8
22	Bargain trainers	N5.10, N5.12, N5.13
23	Fields and rectangles	M4.8, A5.2
24	Handshakes	R4.3, R5.2, R5.8
25	Average scores	HD5.4
26	Cuboid frames	M4.8, S5.8
27	Grid squares	R4.3, R5.2, R5.7
28	Economical boxes	M4.11, A5.3
29	Investigating diagonals	R4.3, R5.8, S5.6
30	Magic shapes	N4.3, R5.7

Oral and mental problem solving starters

Oral and mental activities for the start of each lesson can be selected from this bank of problem solving starters or from other sources.

Children could show their answers using digit cards or fans, individual whiteboards or scraps of paper. This allows less confident children to attempt answers without fear of being incorrect in front of others. It also enables you to survey all children's answers, making a note of common errors or responses from particular individuals.

Allow children time to think about a problem before you expect an answer. You could ask them to wait for a signal from you before they show their answers. This allows all children an equal opportunity to answer questions, not just the quicker or more confident ones.

1 Median and range

(handling data)

The median of three numbers is 6. The range is 8. What could the numbers be? (e.g. 2, 6, 10; 4, 6, 12; 1, 6, 9)

Invite children showing a correct answer to explain how they solved the problem. Note that more able children may give negative or fractional answers.

Repeat with other medians and ranges such as: median 4, range 6 (e.g. 0, 4, 6; 4, 4, 10); median 5, range 8 (e.g. 1, 5, 9; 3, 5, 11); median 10, range 8 (e.g. 2, 10, 10; 6, 10, 14).

2 Continue the sequence

(properties of numbers and number sequences)

Tell children that you are going to say a sequence of numbers. As you go through the sequence, children indicate when they think they know what the pattern is.

Choose individuals to continue the sequence until interest or ability wanes. Ensure that less able children are included early on and the more able at the later stages.

Ask children to describe each pattern.

Sequences could include:

- successive doubling, e.g. 1, 2, 4, 8, 16, 32 . . . ; 3, 6, 12, 24, 48 . . .
- where each number is the sum of the previous 2 numbers, e.g. 0, 1, 1, 2, 3, 5, 8, 13 . . . (Fibonacci sequence); 0, 2, 2, 4, 6, 10 . . .
- differences increasing by 1, e.g. 0, 1, 3, 6, 10, 15 . . .

3 Target 100

(mental calculation strategies + and −)

Give me three 2-digit numbers with a total of 100.

Ask children to explain the strategy they used for finding the numbers. (Likely initial choices will be multiples of 10 such as 20, 10 and 70.) *What if multiples of 10 are not allowed?* What strategies do the children use now?

Eliminate other multiples such as 5 and 2.

4 Target 10

(mental calculation strategies)

How many different ways can you make 10 using the digits 2, 3 and 4?

Answers might include: $(2 \times 3) + 4$; $4 + 3 + 3$; $(4 \times 3) − 2$; $(2 \times 2 \times 2) + 2$

Encourage children to be adventurous, e.g. $(24 \div 2) − 2$; $(32 \div 2) − (2 \times 3)$; $(42 \div 3) − 4$

When recording more complex calculations, ensure children use brackets to indicate the order in which to calculate.

5 Multiplication trio

(mental calculation strategies $\times$ and $\div$)

I multiply 3 numbers together. The answer is 60. What could the numbers be?

Children work in pairs. Give them a few minutes to work out as many possibilities as they can.

Invite children to give you their answers. Discuss any strategies they used. Recommend strategies that are systematic. Whole number possibilities are:

$1 \times 1 \times 60$; $1 \times 2 \times 30$; $1 \times 3 \times 20$; $1 \times 4 \times 15$; $1 \times 5 \times 12$; $1 \times 6 \times 10$; $2 \times 2 \times 15$; $2 \times 3 \times 10$; $2 \times 5 \times 6$; $3 \times 4 \times 5$

Note that more able children may give solutions that include fractions.

Discuss whether using the same numbers in different orders should be counted as different possibilities, e.g. *Is $2 \times 3 \times 10$ the same as $3 \times 10 \times 2$?*

6 Shopping

(mental calculation strategies, money)

Draw shopping items labelled £6.35, £7.18, £15.21 and £2.82. Ask questions such as: *What do I buy? I buy . . . 2 items for £22.39 (£15.21 and £7.18) . . . 2 items with a difference in price of 83p (£7.18 and £6.35) . . . 1 item, give £10 and get £2.82 change (£7.18) . . . 2 items, give £10 and get no change (£7.18 and £2.82) . . . 3 of one item and get 95p change from £20 (£6.35)*

Each time, ask children to explain how they arrived at the answer. Encourage them to look for clues to the answers, rather than doing a complete calculation, e.g. just adding the pence digits or approximating.

7 Apples and pears

(properties of numbers)

Write this problem: *Megan spent £2 on apples and pears. Apples cost 10p and pears cost 20p. She bought twice as many apples as pears. How many of each fruit did she buy?* (5 pears, 10 apples)

Discuss the strategies children used. Recommend strategies that are systematic and involve patterns.

What if Megan bought 3 times as many apples as pears? (4 pears, 12 apples) *. . . twice as many pears as apples?* (8 pears, 4 apples,)

8 All the digits

(properties of numbers)

Write the digits 0, 1, 2, 3, 4, 5, 6, 7, 8 and 9. Children work in pairs. Can they use all the digits once only to make five multiples of 3? Allow them five minutes to do this. Children may find it helpful to use a set of digit cards.

Discuss their strategies and solutions (e.g. 90, 81, 72, 63, 54; 12, 30, 45, 96, 87). Establish that the sum of the digits of a multiple of 3 is divisible by 3.

Can they find a solution that includes a 3-digit number? (e.g. 9, 810, 42, 75, 63)

9 Imaginary shapes

(shape and space)

Have available for demonstration some large paper shapes such as a regular hexagon, a regular pentagon and various quadrilaterals.

Imagine a regular hexagon. Now, in your heads, fold it in half along a line of symmetry. Ask individuals to describe where their fold is. Encourage them to be concise and to use the correct mathematical language. (The fold will either be along an appropriate diagonal or joining the mid-points of opposite sides.)

What shape is each half of the hexagon?

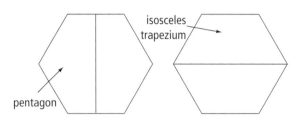

How many different folds could I make to fold the shape in half along a line of symmetry? (6)

Use a paper shape to confirm the answers.

Repeat for other shapes.

10 I'm thinking of a fraction

(fractions)

I'm thinking of a fraction of a number. The answer is 6. What could the fraction and the number be? (e.g. $\frac{1}{4}$ of 24) Encourage more able children to use non-unit fractions (e.g. $\frac{2}{3}$ of 9). Discuss how children arrived at their answers.

Increase the size of the numbers.

11 Stamp shortage!

(properties of numbers and number sequences)

The post office is running out of stamps! It only has 5p, 7p and 9p stamps left. What different amounts can you make using just 3 stamps?

Children work in pairs, writing down their answers. After a few minutes invite children to give you their results and to explain how they tackled the investigation. Write the results on the board. Recommend methods that involve systematically finding all possible combinations, e.g. considering all totals using 5p stamps first, then those that use 7p, then 9p stamps: 5p + 5p + 5p; 5p + 5p + 7p; 5p + 5p + 9p; 5p + 7p + 7p; 5p + 7p + 9p; 5p + 9p + 9p; 7p + 7p + 7p; 7p + 7p + 9p; 7p + 9p + 9p; 9p + 9p + 9p (Possible amounts: 15p, 17p, 19p, 21p, 23p, 25p, 27p.)

12 Punctuality

(measures)

Write this problem: *Jake's driving test is at 9:30 am sharp. His watch is 15 minutes fast. He thinks his watch is 10 minutes fast. Will he be on time for the start of his test?*

Children discuss the problem with a partner. Discuss children's answers and their reasoning. (Jake will be on time.)

Deal with these problems in a similar way: *Mary's driving test is at 9:30 am sharp. Her watch is 15 minutes fast. She thinks her watch is 20 minutes fast. Will she be on time for the start of the test?* (Mary will be late.)

Sara's driving test is at 9:30 am sharp. Her watch is 15 minutes slow. She thinks her watch is 10 minutes fast. Will she be on time for the start of the test? (Sara will be late.)

13 Calendar calculations

(measures)

Ask calendar questions based on the current day, e.g. *Today is Tuesday 4th January . . .*
What will the date be in exactly 3 weeks time? (25th January) *What date was it 31 days ago?* (4th December) *What day will it be in 10 days' time?* (Friday) *What day was it 22 days ago?* (Monday) *What day is 11th January?* (Tuesday) *What day is 9th February?* (Wednesday)

Include questions for more able children such as: *What day will it be on this date next year?* (Wednesday, or Thursday if the last day of February in a leap year is crossed.)

Each time ask children to explain how they worked out the answer.

14 Balanced masses

(mental calculation strategies + and –; measures)

On six cards write 6 masses, e.g. 1.2 kg, 550 g, 2.2 kg, 3.6 kg, 2.7 kg, 8 kg. Choose a pair of cards. Hold one in each hand, with arms outstretched, with the heavier arm downwards, as if you are a pair of scales.

Children write down on pieces of paper the mass that will balance your arms. Choose a child with the correct mass to come and place it in your hand to balance your arms.

Children could play the part of the scales. Extend the activity by having 2 or 3 masses in one hand and 1 or 2 in the other.

15 Doubling up

(mental calculation strategies × and ÷)

Write a small starting number. Children work in pairs to double the number, and then successively double the answers, writing all results down. They double as many times as they can in one minute.

Starting numbers can be integers, decimals or fractions, e.g. 1, 2, 4, 8, 16, 32, 64, 128 . . . ; 0.3, 0.6, 1.2, 2.4, 4.8, 9.6 . . . ; $\frac{1}{20}, \frac{1}{10}, \frac{1}{5}, \frac{2}{5}, \frac{4}{5}, 1\frac{3}{5}, 3\frac{1}{5}$ . . .

Go over the results with the whole class, discussing their strategies for doubling and noting any patterns.

16 What's the calculation?

(mental calculation strategies)

Write on the board 2625 as if in a calculator display.

What 2 numbers and 1 operation could have been keyed in to give this answer? (e.g. 2000 + 625)

Ask similar questions but apply conditions, e.g. *At least one of the numbers must be a 5-digit number* (e.g. 10 000 − 7375) . . . *a decimal* (e.g. 5250 × 0.5). *The operation is multiplication* (e.g. 105 × 25) . . . *division* (e.g. 10 500 ÷ 4).

Discuss how children arrived at their answers. Extend the activity by asking: *What 3 numbers and 2 operations could have been keyed in to give the answer?*

17 Here's the fraction, what's the number?

(fractions)

What's the number if $\frac{3}{4}$ of it is 18? (24) . . . $\frac{3}{8}$ *of it is 6?* (16) . . . $\frac{2}{5}$ *of it is 10?* (25) . . . $\frac{7}{10}$ *of it is 28?* (40) . . . $\frac{5}{6}$ *of it is 50?* (60).

(Note that the given number each time should be a multiple of the numerator.)

Each time discuss how children arrived at their solution.

18 Imaginary multiplication square

(properties of numbers and number sequences)

Ask children to imagine a multiplication square (like the one on PCM 9).

I'm looking at a 16. To the left of it is a 12. What number is to the right of it? (20) What number is underneath it? (20) What number is above it? (12)

Use a multiplication square to confirm their answers. Repeat for other numbers.

19 A long week

(measures; mental calculation strategies)

Is a week longer or shorter than a million seconds?

Discuss children's responses and how they arrived at them. Discuss how the number of seconds in a day, then a week, could be estimated (e.g. $20 \times 60 \times 60 = 72\,000$ for seconds in a day, then $70\,000 \times 7 = 490\,000$ for seconds in a week).

20 Number chains

(properties of numbers and number sequences)

Start with a small number, e.g. 1. Apply a pair of operations to it, for example $\times 2$ then $+2$ ($= 4$). Then apply the same operations to the result and all successive results. Slowly write the resulting sequence on the board: 1, 4, 10, 22, 46 . . .

Children indicate when they think they know what the 2 operations are and continue the sequence.

Let children decide on their own starting numbers and sequences to write on the board.

21 Missing signs

(mental calculation strategies)

Write number sentences with the operations missing, e.g. $64 * 3 * 2 = 134$ ($+$ and $\times$); $36 * 3 * 4 = 8$ ($\div$ and $-$); $54 * 36 * 10 = 80$ ($+$ and $-$); $32 * 10 * 15 = 305$ ($\times$ and $-$).

Children work out what the operations are. Discuss children's methods. (These are likely to involve a combination of approximation, knowledge of properties of numbers, and trial and improvement.)

22 Connected percentages

(fractions, decimals, percentages, ratio and proportion)

Ask children a series of connected percentage questions, whereby the answer to previous questions could help provide the answer to the next, for example by doubling or halving, e.g. *What is 10% of 30? (3) . . . 5% of 30? ($1\frac{1}{2}$ by halving 10% of 30) . . . $2\frac{1}{2}$% of 30? ($\frac{3}{4}$ by halving 5% of 30)*

What is 20% of 30? (6 by doubling 10% of 30) . . . 20% of 60? (12 by doubling 20% of 30) . . . 5% of 60? (3 by halving 20% of 60 twice) . . . $2\frac{1}{2}$% of 60? ($1\frac{1}{2}$ by halving 5% of 60)

What is $7\frac{1}{2}$% of 60? ($4\frac{1}{2}$ by adding 5% and $2\frac{1}{2}$% of 60) . . . 15% of 60? (9 by doubling $7\frac{1}{2}$% of 60)

What is $17\frac{1}{2}$% of 60? ($10\frac{1}{2}$ by doubling 5% of 60 and adding $7\frac{1}{2}$% of 60) . . . $17\frac{1}{2}$% of 30? ($5\frac{1}{4}$ by halving $17\frac{1}{2}$% of 60)

(You may wish to record the questions and answers for use in subsequent questions.) Periodically, ask children to explain how they calculated the answer. You could discuss how such methods are useful for calculating VAT at $17\frac{1}{2}$%.

23 I'm thinking of a rectangle

(measures)

I'm thinking of a rectangle. The area is 375 square centimetres. What could the length and breadth be?

Discuss the possibilities (1 cm $\times$ 375 cm; 3 cm $\times$ 125 cm; 5 cm $\times$ 75 cm; 15 cm $\times$ 25 cm are the whole number possibilities). Ask children to explain how they arrived at their answers. (Methods are likely to include tests of divisibility and factors.) Encourage more able children to consider fractions of a centimetre, e.g. 10 cm $\times$ 37.5 cm; 0.5 cm $\times$ 750 cm.

Repeat for other areas such as 130 cm^2; 215 cm^2; 72 cm^2.

Invite children to be the 'thinkers'.

24 Ten questions

(properties of numbers)

Write down a number less than 1000 on a piece of paper, but don't let the children see it. Children try to track down the number by asking no more than 10 questions with 'yes' or 'no' answers, e.g. *Is it a multiple of 3? Is it even? Is it a 2-digit number? Is it less than 50? Is it divisible by 9?*

After a few games, discuss good strategies, e.g. asking if the number is even eliminates half the numbers straight away.

25 Average guesses

(handling data)

I'm thinking of 3 numbers. Their mean is 50. Their median is 52. What could the numbers be?

Ask children to explain how they arrived at their answers. (The sum of the 3 numbers must be 150. So the sum of the 2 unknown numbers must be $150 - 52 = 98$. So possibilities are 0 and 98, 1 and 97, 2 and 96, 3 and 95 . . . 46 and 52.)

Discuss the possibilities of decimal numbers.

Repeat with other data, e.g. *I'm thinking of 3 numbers. Their mean is 70. Their median is 4. What could the 3 numbers be?*

26 I'm thinking of a box

(measures)

I'm thinking of a cuboid box. It will hold exactly 40 centimetre cubes. What are the length, breadth and height of the box?

Elicit all possible answers (40 cm, 1 cm, 1 cm; 20 cm, 2 cm, 1 cm; 10 cm, 4 cm, 1 cm; 10 cm, 2 cm, 2 cm; 8 cm, 5 cm, 1 cm; 5 cm, 4 cm, 2 cm).

Discuss approaches to the problem. Recommend systematic approaches.

Repeat for other cuboids such as ones that will hold 60, 50 or 72 centimetre cubes.

27 Squares

(properties of numbers and number sequences; using a calculator)

Write 625. *Which number when multiplied by itself results in 625?* (25) Children use calculators to find the answer. (If there is a square root key, they are not allowed to use it.)

Children explain how they worked out the answer.

Repeat for other square numbers such as 729 (27^2), 1296 (36^2), 1681 (41^2), 2809 (53^2).

28 Surface areas

(measures)

The surface area of a cuboid with a square cross-section is 56 cm². The square faces have sides of 2 cm. What is the length of the cuboid? (6 cm)

Children work in pairs. Allow them a few minutes to find the solution. Discuss their strategies. (These are likely to involve: subtracting the surface area of the 2 square faces from the total surface area to get the surface area of the 4 rectangular faces; dividing the result by 4 to obtain the surface area of one rectangular face; dividing that result by 2 to find the length.)

Repeat with a similar problem such as: *The surface area of a cuboid with a square cross-section is 102 cm². The square faces have sides of 3 cm. What is the length of the cuboid?* (7 cm)

29 Digits 1 to 4

(mental calculation strategies)

Children use the digits 1 to 4 and operating signs to make as many numbers as they can from 1 onwards. Each digit can be used no more than once in each expression. There is no limit to the number of times operating signs can be used. Write an expression by the side of each number, e.g. $1 = 4 - 3$; $2 = 3 - 1$; $3 = 1 + 2$; $4 = 1 + 3$; $5 = 4 + 2 - 1$; $6 = 2 \times 3$; $7 = (2 \times 4) - 1$; $8 = 2 \times 4$; $9 = 3^2$; $10 = 3^2 + 1$

You could make a display of children's solutions for each number. This could be added to over time.

30 Banned keys

(mental calculation strategies; using a calculator)

Children use calculators. They calculate 78×36 but they are not allowed to use the $\boxed{6}$ key. Discuss the strategies children used, e.g.
$78 \times 35 + 78 =$ or $78 \times 72 \div 2 =$

Repeat the calculation with $\boxed{7}$, $\boxed{8}$, $\boxed{\times}$ or $\boxed{3}$ as the banned keys.

Repeat with other calculations.

1 Cycle tour

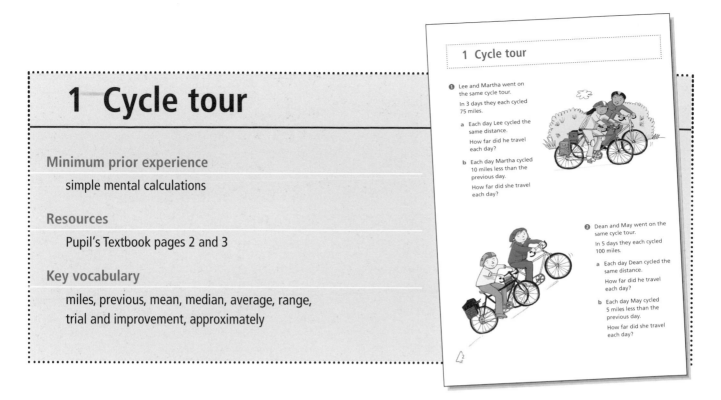

Minimum prior experience

simple mental calculations

Resources

Pupil's Textbook pages 2 and 3

Key vocabulary

miles, previous, mean, median, average, range, trial and improvement, approximately

What's the problem?

An arithmetical problem involving distances in miles, reasoning about numbers, trial and improvement methods and possibly finding the mean, median and range. There is the opportunity for the More able group to apply an algebraic approach.

Problem solving objectives

- Choose and use appropriate number operations to solve problems and appropriate ways of calculating.

- Solve mathematical problems or puzzles, recognise and explain patterns and relationships, generalise and predict. Suggest extensions asking 'What if . . . ?'

- Identify and use appropriate operations to solve word problems involving numbers and quantities based on 'real life', money or measures, using one or more steps.
  Explain methods and reasoning.

Differentiation

More able: Pupil's Textbook page 3, problem 4

Average: Pupil's Textbook page 3, problem 3 (similar, but with less demanding numbers and a discretionary clue)

Less able: Pupil's Textbook page 2, problems 1 and 2 (similar, but with more direction and less demanding numbers)

Introducing the problem

Discuss cycling with children. *Who has a bike? How much do you cycle? How far do you think you travel in a week? How far do you think you could cycle in a day?*

Set the context of the problem: cycling tours over several days covering large distances.

Let children read through the problems and ask any questions. Make sure they understand the meaning of 'cycled so many miles less than the previous day'.

Teacher focus for activity

All children: There are several approaches to these problems, from trial and improvement to more calculated approaches. Do not suggest any particular approach, but stimulate children's thinking through questioning: *Can you explain how you are tackling this problem? What do you estimate the distances travelled each day to be? What do the distances have to add up to? What do you think the distance will be on the middle day of the tour? Why? What is the difference between distances travelled on the first and last days (the range of distances)?*

Average: (discretionary clue) *Would it help if you found the mean (average) distance travelled each day? How would that help?*

Less able: Help children to see that **1a** and **2a** provide a baseline distance for each day, which can then be adjusted through trial and improvement to solve **1b** and **2b**.

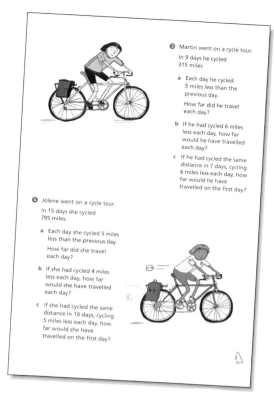

3 Martin went on a cycle tour. In 9 days he cycled 315 miles.

  a Each day he cycled 5 miles less than the previous day. How far did he travel each day?

  b If he had cycled 6 miles less each day, how far would he have travelled each day?

  c If he had cycled the same distance in 7 days, cycling 6 miles less each day, how far would he have travelled on the first day?

4 Jolene went on a cycle tour. In 15 days she cycled 795 miles.

  a Each day she cycled 5 miles less than the previous day. How far did she travel each day?

  b If she had cycled 4 miles less each day, how far would she have travelled each day?

  c If she had cycled the same distance in 10 days, cycling 5 miles less each day, how far would she have travelled on the first day?

Optional adult input

Work with the Less able group. Help children to develop a trial and improvement approach to **1b** and **2b**.

Plenary

1 **Write the first part of problem 3 on the board.** Invite all children to explain the methods they used (or would use) to solve the problem. Encourage them to describe methods they tried and discarded as well as the successful strategies. Throughout, get children to explain the reasoning behind what they did. (*Why did you do that?*) Encourage other children to comment and ask questions.

There are several possible approaches to the problem. Here are two. (See **Useful mathematical information page 82** for an algebraic approach.)

  ● Trial and improvement

   This might involve making a rough guess at the distance travelled on the first day and then repeatedly subtracting 6 to arrive at the mileage for each of the other days. Then adjustments can be made until the total is 315 miles. For example, guessing that the first day's mileage might be 65 miles results in:

   65, 59, 53, 47, 41, 35, 29, 23 and 17 miles

   The total is 369, which is 54 miles more than the required 315 miles.

If we share the excess mileage between the 9 days and subtract the result from each daily mileage, we arrive at the answer, i.e.

$54 \div 9 = 6$ and subtracting 6 from each estimate results in:

   59, 53, 47, 41, 35, 29, 23, 17 and 11 miles (total 315 miles)

  ● Using the mean

Because the distances travelled each day will form an ordered set of numbers with an equal difference between adjacent numbers, then the middle (fifth) number, as well as being the median, will also be the mean.

We can find the mean distance by dividing the total mileage by 9:

   $315 \div 9 = 35$ miles

So on the fifth day, Martin cycled 35 miles.

Now all we need to do is generate the mileages on either side by successively adding or subtracting 6 miles:

   59, 53, 47, 41, **35**, 29, 23, 17 and 11 miles

2 Discuss any difficulties the children might have had with the mathematics. These might include dividing 795 by 15 in problem 4. (See **Useful mathematical information page 82** for three methods of long division.)

Development

Children work on the same problems, investigating the effect of changing the daily reduction in mileage, then the number of days cycled.

Solutions

1 a 25 miles   **b** 35, 25 and 15 miles
2 a 20 miles   **b** 30, 25, 20, 15 and 10 miles

3 a 55, 50, 45, 40, 35, 30, 25, 20 and 15 miles
  b 59, 53, 47, 41, 35, 29, 23, 17 and 11 miles
  c 63 miles

4 a 88, 83, 78, 73, 68, 63, 58, 53, 48, 43, 38, 33, 28, 23 and 18 miles
  b 81, 77, 73, 69, 65, 61, 57, 53, 49, 45, 41, 37, 33, 29 and 25 miles
  c 102 miles

2 Queue jumping

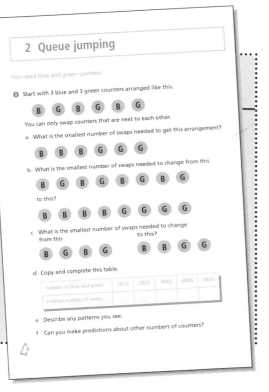

You need blue and green counters.

1 Start with 3 blue and 3 green counters arranged like this.

B G B G B G

You can only swap counters that are next to each other.

a What is the smallest number of swaps needed to get this arrangement?

B B B G G G

b What is the smallest number of swaps needed to change from this

B G B G B G B G

to this?

B B B B G G G G

c What is the smallest number of swaps needed to change from this   to this?

B G B G   B B G G

d Copy and complete this table.

number of blue and green	1B1G	2B2G	3B3G	4B4G	5B5G
smallest number of swaps					

e Describe any patterns you see.

f Can you make predictions about other numbers of counters?

4

What's the problem?

An algebraic investigation that involves working systematically, identifying number patterns and relationships, and using these to make a generalisation in words or as a formula,

Problem solving objectives

- Explain methods and reasoning, orally and in writing.
- Solve mathematical problems or puzzles, recognise and explain patterns and relationships, generalise and predict. Suggest extensions asking 'What if . . . ?'
- Develop from explaining a generalised relationship in words to expressing it in a formula using letters as symbols.

Differentiation

More able: Pupil's Textbook page 5, question 4

Average: Pupil's Textbook page 5, questions 2 and 3 (same problem but with more direction, and describing relationships in words rather than as a formula)

Less able: Pupil's Textbook page 4, question 1 (same problem, but using counters and pictorial help and with less specific expectations for predictions). If appropriate, children could move on to question 2.

Introducing the problem

Use the top of Textbook page 5 to go over the conditions for the investigation. Demonstrate with a small group of children the only way in which

movements can be made: swapping adjacent positions. Point out to the Less able group that their problem is the same except that they are investigating with blue and green counters instead of with boys and girls.

Teacher focus for activity

All children: All children may find it helpful to use counters.

Show me the swaps you used. Are you sure that is the smallest number of swaps possible? How do you know? How many swaps do you think it will take for the next number of boys and girls? Why do you think that?

After investigating 'queues' of 4, 6 and 8, ask children if they have developed a general system of making the swaps. Can they describe it? *Can you describe the pattern in the 'fewest swaps' sequence of numbers? Have you seen this pattern before?* Some children may recognise the numbers as triangular numbers (see **Useful mathematical information pages 82–83**).

More able: For children who appear to be making random investigations, ask: *How could you make your investigation more systematic? How can you organise your work to help find any patterns that might be developing?*

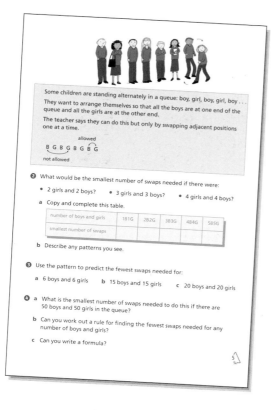

Some children are standing alternately in a queue: boy, girl, boy, girl, boy . . .
They want to arrange themselves so that all the boys are at one end of the queue and all the girls are at the other end.
The teacher says they can do this but only by swapping adjacent positions one at a time.

allowed

B G B G B G B G

not allowed

2 What would be the smallest number of swaps needed if there were:
- 2 girls and 2 boys?
- 3 girls and 3 boys?
- 4 girls and 4 boys?

a Copy and complete this table.

number of boys and girls	1B1G	2B2G	3B3G	4B4G	5B5G
smallest number of swaps					

b Describe any patterns you see.

3 Use the pattern to predict the fewest swaps needed for:
a 6 boys and 6 girls   **b** 15 boys and 15 girls   **c** 20 boys and 20 girls

4 a What is the smallest number of swaps needed to do this if there are 50 boys and 50 girls in the queue?
b Can you work out a rule for finding the fewest swaps needed for any number of boys and girls?
c Can you write a formula?

Optional adult input

Work with the More able group. Ask children to explain what they have discovered in their investigations so far and what they are going to do next.

Plenary

1 **Draw on the board the table from Textbook page 5**

Establish that a good starting point for this investigation would be 1 boy and 1 girl.

How many swaps are needed to arrange all the boys at one end and girls at the other end? (Enter zero in the table.)

Invite 2 boys and 2 girls to the front and arrange them boy, girl, boy, girl. Invite children to demonstrate the minimum number of swaps needed to arrange the boys at one end of the line and the girls at the other. (Enter 1 in the table.)

B G B G ⟶ B B G G

Similarly repeat for 3 boys and 3 girls (3 swaps).

B G B G B G ⟶ B B G G B G ⟶

⟶ B B G B G G ⟶ B B B G G G

then for 4 boys and 4 girls (6 swaps) and 5 boys and 5 girls (10 swaps).

2 *Can you describe the pattern of numbers in the bottom row of the table?* Establish that the difference between consecutive numbers increases by 1 each time. Children may also recognise the numbers as the triangular numbers (see **Useful mathematical information pages 82–83**).

Can you use the pattern to predict the number of swaps needed for 6 boys and 6 girls? (15) . . . *7 boys and 7 girls?* (21) . . . *15 boys and 15 girls?* (105) *How did you work it out?*

3 Ask if anyone managed to work out a way of finding out the minimum number of swaps needed for any number of children. Here is one possibility: Multiply the number of boys (or girls) by one less than the number of boys (or girls) and divide by 2, e.g. for 5 boys and 5 girls: multiply 5 by 4 (20) and divide by 2 (10).

As a formula, this could be written as $N \times (N - 1) \div 2$, where N is the number of boys or girls.

4 Remind children that in this lesson they have been investigating patterns systematically in order to make predictions.

Development

Introduce teachers into the line, e.g. BGTBGTBGT. Ask: *What is the minimum number of moves to sort them so that all boys are together, all teachers are together and all girls are together?*

Solutions

1 a 3   **b** 6   **c** 1   **d** See 2a   **e** See 2b
f Children's own predictions for other numbers of counters

2 a

number of boys and girls	1B1G	2B2G	3B3G	4B4G	5B5G
smallest number of swaps	0	1	3	6	10

b The difference between consecutive swap numbers increases by 1 each time; they are the triangular numbers.

3 a 15   **b** 105   **c** 190
4 a 1225 swaps
b Multiply the number of boys (or girls) by one less than the number of boys (or girls) and divide by 2.
c $N \times (N - 1) \div 2$

3 Dartboards

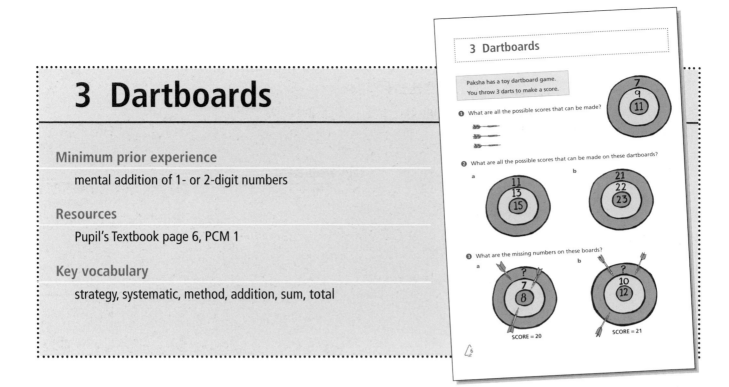

3 Dartboards

Paksha has a toy dartboard game.
You throw 3 darts to make a score.

❶ What are all the possible scores that can be made?

❷ What are all the possible scores that can be made on these dartboards?

a   b

❸ What are the missing numbers on these boards?

a   b

SCORE = 20   SCORE = 21

Minimum prior experience

mental addition of 1- or 2-digit numbers

Resources

Pupil's Textbook page 6, PCM 1

Key vocabulary

strategy, systematic, method, addition, sum, total

What's the problem?

An investigation of numbers and possible totals, requiring systematic working, devising strategies, reasoning about numbers, and mental calculations.

Problem solving objectives

- Choose and use appropriate number operations to solve problems and appropriate ways of calculating.
- Explain methods and reasoning, orally and in writing.
- Solve mathematical problems or puzzles, recognise and explain patterns and relationships, generalise and predict. Suggest extensions asking 'What if . . . ?'

Differentiation

More able: PCM 1 Dartboards 2

Average: PCM 1 Dartboards 1 (same problem, differentiation by outcome and the inclusion of a clue)

Less able: Pupil's Textbook page 6 (similar, but less demanding problems)

Introducing the problem

Give children time to read through the problems and to ask any questions. Explain that it is assumed that all 3 darts actually land in a ring and also that more than one dart can land in any one ring. Encourage children to be systematic and to record what they do. Tell them that there is a definite strategy that will help them solve the problems, if only they can find it!

Teacher focus for activity

More able and Average: Even if children are just trying various combinations of numbers, encourage them to be systematic about it.

As children work, ask questions such as: *How did you start? Why did you start there? How did you work out the numbers?*

For children in the Average group who seem not to be progressing, you could offer this clue: *What if the 3 darts landed in the same ring? What could you tell me about the score?*

For children who have found a solution, ask: *Could there be another solution?* (no) *Why?*

Less able: For questions 1 and 2, encourage children to be systematic rather than just adding random combinations of numbers, e.g. with question 1, starting with all possible combinations that include 7 (7, 7, 7; 7, 7, 9; 7, 7, 11; 7, 9, 9; 7, 9, 11; 7, 11, 11), then investigating all combinations that contain 9; then 11.

Check that children notice that some different combinations give the same total.

Optional adult input

Work with the Less able group, ensuring that children find all possible scores in questions 1 and 2: *How do you know that you have found all the possible scores?* Help them to reason about the answers to question 3, e.g. *What is the score so far?*

Plenary

1 Briefly focus on question 1 on Textbook page 6. **Draw the dartboard on the board.**

Ask children from the Less able group to explain how they found all possible scores. Emphasise the importance of being systematic so that no combinations are omitted.

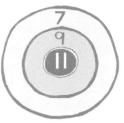

Establish that one systematic way is to deal with all combinations that include 7, then 9, then 11: 7, 7, 7; 7, 7, 9; 7, 7, 11; 7, 9, 9; 7, 9, 11; 7, 11, 11; 9, 9, 9; 9, 9, 11; 9, 11, 11; 11, 11, 11 giving totals of, respectively, 21, 23, 25, 25, 27, 29, 27, 29, 31, 33.

How many possible scores are there? What 3 numbers give the biggest/smallest scores? (11, 11, 11/7, 7, 7)

2 Now focus on PCM 1. **Draw the blank dartboard on the board and the 10 possible scores: 9, 13, 16, 17, 20, 21, 23, 24, 27, 30.**

Invite any children who have found the solution to write the 3 numbers on the blank dartboard. Together with the class, check that the solution is correct.

Ask children to explain how they arrived at a solution. As they explain, make sure that they give the reasoning behind what they did. (*Why did you do that?*)

One approach to the solution is as follows. If not covered in children's methods, you could go over it using a series of questions:

- *What is the largest score?* (30)

- *Where would the darts need to land to get a score of 30?* (3 darts in the ring with the biggest number)

- *So if 3 darts in the biggest number give a score of 30, what must the number be?* (Establish that the largest dartboard number must be 10.)

- *What is the smallest score?* (9)

- *Where would the darts need to land to get a score of 9?* (3 darts in the ring with the smallest number)

- *So if 3 darts in the smallest number give a score of 9, what must the number be?* (Establish that the smallest dartboard number must be 3.)

- *How could we find out what the third number is?*

- *What is the second biggest possible score?* (27)

- *Where would the 3 darts have to land to get the second biggest score?* (2 in the largest number and 1 in the second largest number)

- Establish that two darts in the largest number would give 10 + 10 = 20. So the other number must be 7.

The three numbers then are 3, 7 and 10.

Development

Children make up similar problems for each other to solve, using 3- and 4-ring dartboards.

Solutions

PCM 1
3, 7, 10; 2, 9, 11

Textbook page 6
1 21, 23, 25, 27, 29, 31, 33
2 a 33, 35, 37, 39, 41, 43, 45
  b 63, 64, 65, 66, 67, 68, 69
3 a 6
  b 7

4 Magic squares

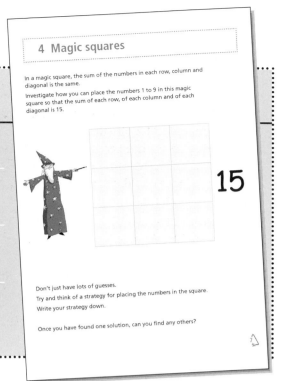

4 Magic squares

In a magic square, the sum of the numbers in each row, column and diagonal is the same.

Investigate how you can place the numbers 1 to 9 in this magic square so that the sum of each row, of each column and of each diagonal is 15.

15

Don't just have lots of guesses.
Try and think of a strategy for placing the numbers in the square.
Write your strategy down.

Once you have found one solution, can you find any others?

Minimum prior experience

mental addition of 1- and 2-digit numbers

Resources

Pupil's Textbook page 7, PCM 2, squared paper

Key vocabulary

row, column, diagonal, strategy, total, sum, pattern, because, therefore, if . . . then

What's the problem?

Reasoning and generalising about numbers to solve traditional 3 × 3 magic squares.

Problem solving objectives

- Explain methods and reasoning, orally and in writing.
- Solve mathematical problems or puzzles, recognise and explain patterns and relationships, generalise and predict. Suggest extensions asking 'What if . . . ?'

Differentiation

More able: Pupil's Textbook page 7

Average: Pupil's Textbook page 7 (same problem, but with a discretionary clue)

Less able: PCM 2 (filling in the missing numbers in incomplete magic squares)

Introducing the problem

Allow children to read through their problems. Establish the features of a magic square.

Explain to children doing the Textbook activity that it may be possible to find a solution by randomly trying numbers in different positions. Initially they may need to do this to help them think about the problem, but explain that you are interested in whether they can reason about the numbers in the square and any strategies they use to arrive at a solution. They should record for the plenary what they do and think as they work.

Teacher focus for activity

More able and Average: Initially children may need to randomly try numbers in different positions in the square. However, encourage them to start thinking about the numbers and the various positions in the square. For children who are finding it difficult to get started, you could ask questions to get them thinking: *What is the sum of all the numbers in this row/column/ diagonal? What could the numbers be? What else could they be? Is there anything about the middle position that is different from the others? What can you tell me about the corner positions? What about the 'side' positions?*

Average: (discretionary clue) *What are all the possibilities for making a total of 15 using three numbers from 1 to 9?*

Less able: *Which position in the square are you going to work out first? Why? Will that help you get another number? How? Then what will you do? Why?*

Optional adult input

Work with the Less able group, asking children the questions suggested in the **Teacher focus for activity**.

Plenary

1 **Draw the first two partially completed magic squares from PCM 2 on the board.**

Ask children from the Less able group to help you complete them, discussing the order in which the first few squares could be completed and how each number could be calculated.

2 **Draw a blank 3 × 3 square on the board.**

Focus on Textbook page 7. Explain that at this stage you are interested, not in the solution itself, but in strategies for finding a solution.

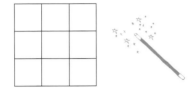

Invite children who used a strategy for finding the solution to explain the strategy to the others.

Discuss each strategy and the reasoning behind it. (*Why did you do that?*)

If it has not already been given, offer the following strategy:

- *It would be useful to find all the possibilities for making a total of 15 using three numbers from 1 to 9. How could we do this systematically?* One systematic approach is to fix one of the numbers as 1 and investigate what other pairs of numbers with it will make 15. Then fix one of the numbers as 2, then 3, and so on. This will result in the following 8 different possibilities:

  $1 + 5 + 9$; $1 + 6 + 8$; $2 + 4 + 9$; $2 + 5 + 8$;
  $2 + 6 + 7$; $3 + 4 + 8$; $3 + 5 + 7$; $4 + 5 + 6$

  Point out that there are 8 possible addition combinations and, conveniently, there are 8 additions involved in the magic square (3 horizontal, 3 vertical, 2 diagonal).

- *How many additions is the centre number of the square involved in?* (4: 1 vertical, 1 horizontal and 2 diagonal) *So what could the centre number be?* Establish that the centre number must be 5 because 5 is the only number that appears in four of the addition combinations above. Write '5' in the square.

- Establish similarly that each corner number is involved in 3 additions (1 vertical, 1 horizontal and 1 diagonal). The numbers that are involved in only three addition combinations are 2, 4, 6 and 8. So the corner numbers must be 2, 4, 6 and 8. Write the corner numbers in the square.

Does it matter which corners the numbers go in? Why/why not? (For diagonal totals of 15, opposite corners must add up to 10, so 2 and 8 must be in diagonally opposite corners, as must 6 and 4.)

- Discuss the remaining numbers 1, 3, 7 and 9, which must be the side numbers. Note that side numbers are involved in only 2 additions and appear in only 2 of the addition combinations. The side numbers can now be positioned.

  Ask children to check that each addition combination above appears in the square.

3 Point out that this problem was solved through reasoning and being systematic.

Development

Children use the magic square as a base for creating others, e.g. can they devise a magic square that uses the first 9 even numbers . . . a fraction magic square . . . a decimal magic square?

Solutions

Textbook page 7
This is one solution. There are 7 other solutions that are reflections or rotations of this square.

8	3	4
1	5	9
6	7	2

PCM 2

1

3	8	1
2	4	6
7	0	5

2

5	10	3
4	6	8
9	2	7

3

80	30	40
10	50	90
60	70	20

4

12	2	16
14	10	6
4	18	8

5 Children's own answers based on one of the previous magic squares with all its numbers multiplied by 2.

5 Multiplication investigation

Minimum prior experience

understanding multiplication; quick recall of multiplication facts; mental addition of several 1- or 2-digit numbers

Resources

Pupil's Textbook pages 8 and 9, large copy of diagrams from the Textbook pages, scrap paper, calculators (discretionary)

Key vocabulary

total, product, adjacent, investigate, adjust, trial and improvement, strategy

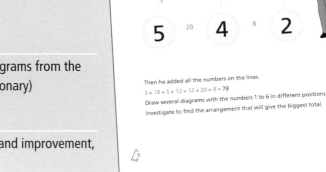

5 Multiplication investigation

Jake drew a diagram like this.
He put each number from 1 to 6 in a circle.
He multiplied adjacent numbers and wrote the answers on the lines that joined them.

1   3   3   18   6

5   12   12

5   20   4   8   2

Then he added all the numbers on the lines.
3 + 18 + 5 + 12 + 12 + 20 + 8 = 78
Draw several diagrams with the numbers 1 to 6 in different positions.
Investigate to find the arrangement that will give the biggest total.

What's the problem?

A mathematical puzzle involving reasoning about numbers, trial and improvement methods, recalling multiplication facts and adding several 1- and 2-digit numbers.

Problem solving objectives

- Explain methods and reasoning, orally and in writing.
- Solve mathematical problems or puzzles, recognise and explain patterns and relationships, generalise and predict. Suggest extensions asking 'What if . . . ?'

Differentiation

More able: Pupil's Textbook page 9

Average: Pupil's Textbook page 8 (similar problem but using fewer numbers)

Less able: Pupil's Textbook page 8 (same problem as for Average, but with discretionary use of calculators and further differentiation through outcome)

Introducing the problem

Explain to children that in this lesson they will be doing a number puzzle involving facts from the multiplication tables and mental addition of several 1- or 2-digit numbers. Allow children to read through the instructions, and ensure that they understand what is required. Explain that they should use scrap paper to make their investigations, although their final diagram and addition sentence should be clearly presented (give children a few minutes before the plenary to do this).

Teacher focus for activity

All children: To encourage children to think about strategies for positioning numbers, ask questions such as: *How many numbers is that position multiplied by? Why have you put that number there? What difference would it make if you swapped these numbers round? Is it better to put a larger number in this position or a smaller one? Why?*

If children cannot instantly recall a particular multiplication fact, encourage them to derive it from a fact they already know. When adding the final string of numbers, encourage them to look for quick mental methods.

Average and Less able: To help children think strategically, use sections of a diagram or less complex diagrams, e.g. ask children to investigate positioning numbers in these diagrams:

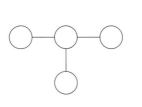

(using numbers 1 to 4)   (using numbers 1 to 5)

Optional adult input

Work with the Less able group using simpler diagrams and questions as suggested in **Teacher focus for activity**.

2 Li drew a diagram like this.

She put each number from 1 to 9 in a circle.

She multiplied adjacent numbers and wrote the answers on the lines that joined them.

```
3   18   6   30   5
  21      6       20
7    7   1    4   4
  56      2       36
8   16   2   18   9
```

Then she added all the numbers on the lines.

18 + 30 + 21 + 6 + 20 + 7 + 4 + 56 + 2 + 36 + 16 + 18 = **234**

Draw several diagrams with the numbers 1 to 9 in different positions.

Investigate to find the arrangement that will give the biggest total.

9

Plenary

Display a large copy of each diagram.

1 Focus first on Textbook page 8.

Ask children to describe key points of the strategies they used and discuss them. These are likely to include the fact that the 2 central circles involve 3 multiplications whereas the corner circles involve only 2. *Is it better to put larger or smaller numbers in the central circles? Why?*

Invite children to give their highest total. Ask a child with the highest total to write the numbers in the circles.

As a class, work out the products of adjacent numbers and write them on the lines. Write all the line numbers underneath the diagram as an addition sentence. Discuss possible strategies for adding the numbers, e.g. looking for near doubles or pairs of numbers that make a multiple of 10. Ask children to work out the total. Point out that there may be other ways of arriving at this total.

If the total is less than 100 explain that it is not the highest possible total; suggest that children could continue the investigation to find a bigger total.

2 Deal with Textbook page 9 in a similar way. During discussions establish that the central circle involves 4 multiplications, the 4 corner circles involve 2 each, and the remaining 4 circles involve 3. Discuss the best numbers to insert in the different types of circle.

If the highest total produced is less than 371 suggest that children could continue the investigation to find a bigger total.

Development

Children investigate the arrangement of numbers that will produce the smallest total.

Solutions

Here is one arrangement for each diagram, giving the biggest totals. There are others.

Textbook page 8

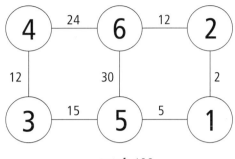

```
4   24   6   12   2
12       30       2
3   15   5    5   1
```

total: 100

Textbook page 9

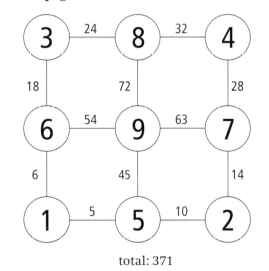

```
3   24   8   32   4
18       72       28
6   54   9   63   7
6        45       14
1    5   5   10   2
```

total: 371

6 Financial fudge

6 Financial fudge

❶ Maria makes 5 slabs of fudge.
She cuts each slab into 6 rows and 10 columns.

  a How many pieces of fudge does she get?

Maria puts the pieces of fudge into bags of 20 pieces.

  b How many bags does she fill?

Maria sells each bag for 50p.

  c How much money does she get if she sells all the bags?

Maria paid £5 for the ingredients.

  d If she sells all the bags, how much profit does she make altogether?

❷ If Maria made 6 slabs of fudge using the same ingredients, how much profit would she make altogether?

10

Minimum prior experience

multiplication, division, addition and subtraction of 2-digit numbers; money calculations

Resources

Pupil's Textbook pages 10 and 11

Key vocabulary

profit, costs, method, strategy

What's the problem?

'Real-life' multi-step problems involving all 4 operations and money, requiring children to select appropriate operations, methods of calculation and checking strategies.

Problem solving objectives

- Choose and use appropriate number operations to solve problems and appropriate ways of calculating.
- Identify and use appropriate operations to solve word problems involving numbers and quantities based on 'real life', money or measures, using one or more steps.
  Explain methods and reasoning.

Differentiation

More able: Pupil's Textbook page 11

Average: Pupil's Textbook page 11 (same problem, but with discretionary 'leading' questions)

Less able: Pupil's Textbook page 10 (similar problem, but with a more structured set of questions and less demanding numbers)

Introducing the problem

Allow children time to read through the problems and to ask any questions. Remind them that they should record their working clearly so that you can see how they tackled the problem. They should start working on the problem straight away.

Teacher focus for activity

All children: As children work, ask them to explain what they have done so far and what they intend to do next.

Ask children to explain the method they used for particular calculations: a mental or written method or a combination of both. Encourage them to suggest and demonstrate strategies for checking their answers.

The numbers involved in some calculations may be out of the range of those they have previously experienced. In such cases, encourage children to devise their own methods of making the calculations.

Average: (discretionary) For children who are 'stuck' at a particular stage in the problem, ask 'leading' questions to help them progress, e.g. *How much did he sell all the bags for? What do you need to know? How could you find that out? How many bags of fudge did he make? What do you need to know? How could you find that out? What information on page 11 is not needed to answer this question?*

Optional adult input

Work with the Less able group. Ensure that the answer to each question is correct before children progress to the next question.

Imran makes 6 slabs of fudge for the school fête.

Each slab is 1.5 cm thick.

He paid £12.16 for the ingredients.

He cuts each slab of fudge into 16 rows and 12 columns.

He puts the pieces of fudge into bags of 15, eating any leftover pieces.

Each bag weighs 250 g.

He sells each bag for 56p. He sells all the bags.

What profit does Imran make on each bag of fudge?

BOOKS

☆ FUDGE ☆

Plenary

1 Start by using Textbook page 10 to establish a method for calculating profit, then focus on Textbook page 11.

Establish that the problem is to calculate the profit made on each bag of fudge and that the thickness of the fudge slabs and the weight of the bags are bogus information.

Invite individuals to describe the steps they took in solving the problem. Compare these with the method used in the problem on Textbook page 10. Write each step on the board. One possibility is:

- Work out the number of fudge pieces in one slab. ($16 \times 12 = 192$)

- Work out the total number of fudge pieces. ($192 \times 6 = 1152$)

- Find out how many bags of fudge were filled. ($1152 \div 15 = 76$ r 12, so Imran filled 76 bags and ate the 12 fudge pieces left over)

- Calculate the money made from the sale of the bags. ($76 \times 56p = 4256p = £42.56$)

- Work out the total profit. ($£42.56 - £12.16 = £30.40$)

- Work out the profit on each bag. ($£30.40 \div 76 = £0.40$ or 40p)

An alternative from the third step onwards is:

- Calculate the cost of the ingredients for each bag. ($£12.16 \div 76 = £0.16$ or 16p)

- Work out the profit on each bag. ($56p - 16p = 40p$)

Emphasise the fact that problems can be solved in different ways.

2 Discuss the methods children used to do each calculation, e.g.

- The answer to 16×12 could be found mentally by multiplying 16 by 10 (160), multiplying 16 by 2 (32) and adding the two answers (192), or a standard written method or a grid method could be used (see **Useful mathematical information page 83**).

- The answer to $£42.56 - £12.16$ can easily be done mentally because each digit on the left is larger than or equal to the corresponding digit on the right, so no exchange is involved.

Some calculations are more difficult and methods used should be discussed, e.g.

- $1152 \div 15$

  There are several ways in which this calculation could be done, including a standard written method or a subtraction or 'building up' method. For an example of each method see **Useful mathematical information page 82**.

- 76×56

  A standard written method could be used for this calculation or a grid method (see **Useful mathematical information page 83**). It could also be done using a combination of mental and written methods, e.g. multiply 76 by 100 and halve ($7600 \div 2 = 3800$); multiply 76 by 6 using a written method ($76 \times 6 = 456$); add the two answers ($3800 + 456 = 4256$).

- $£12.16 \div 76$

  The amount could be changed to pence (1216p) and then divided using a standard written method of long division or a subtraction or 'building up' method (see **Useful mathematical information page 82**).

Development

Children find a recipe for a cake or something else that they could make for a school fête. They research ingredient costs, decide how much they could sell the items for and calculate the profit they could make.

Solutions

1 a 300 pieces   **b** 15 bags   **c** £7.50   **d** £2.50

2 £4

3 40p profit on each bag

33

7 Marco's pizzeria

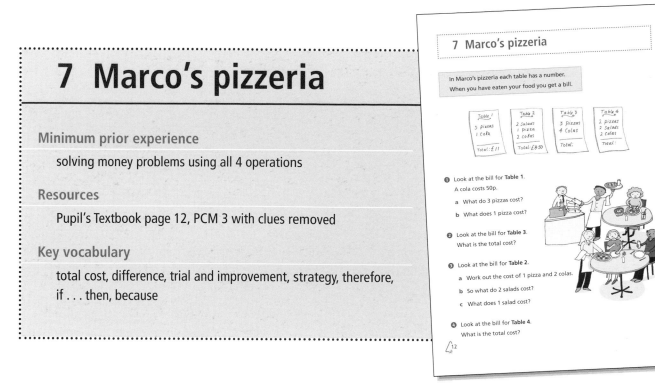

Minimum prior experience

solving money problems using all 4 operations

Resources

Pupil's Textbook page 12, PCM 3 with clues removed

Key vocabulary

total cost, difference, trial and improvement, strategy, therefore, if . . . then, because

---

What's the problem?

Essentially algebraic 'real-life' problems that involve finding unknown costs from known costs in the context of a pizzeria.

Problem solving objectives

- Choose and use appropriate number operations to solve problems and appropriate ways of calculating.
- Identify and use appropriate operations to solve word problems involving numbers and quantities based on 'real life', money or measures, using one or more steps.
Explain methods and reasoning.

Differentiation

More able: PCM 3

Average: PCM 3 (same problem but using clues where necessary)

Less able: Pupil's Textbook page 12 (same problem, but with more guidance given)

Introducing the problem

Set the scene by talking about restaurants and discussing children's experiences of restaurants and restaurant bills. Explain that in this lesson they will be solving problems about prices and bills in a pizzeria. Remind children that they should record how they solved a problem as well as the answer.

Tell children that they should first look very carefully at the problem and discuss with each other ways of solving it.

Teacher focus for activity

Allow children at least 5 minutes to discuss the problem before you make any interventions.

All children: To help children clarify what they need to do, ask questions such as: *What is the problem asking? What data are you given? What do you need to find out first? How could you find that out?*

More able: For those who are finding it difficult to get started, suggest that they focus on the bills for Tables 1 and 3 to find the cost of one of the items.

Average: Provide Clue 1 and then Clue 2 (from the bottom of PCM 3) to children who appear to be making no headway.

Optional adult input

Work with the Average group. Get children to check answers to individual calculations. *How could you check that this is right?*

Plenary

1 Focus on PCM 3.

Ask children for their solutions. Ask one or two children with a correct answer (£12) to explain the problem solving strategy they used. Ensure that other children understand the strategy and encourage them to ask questions. During the explanation, take opportunities to involve children from the Less able group, pointing out the relevant question on Textbook page 12 that is being considered at each stage. For example, ask: *What did you work out the cost of 3 pizzas to be?* (question 1) *What about the cost of 1 pizza? How did you do that? What did you work out the cost of 1 pizza and 2 colas to be?* (question 3) *How could we work out the cost of a salad?*

Successful strategies for PCM 3 are likely to be along the following lines:

- Focus on the bills for Tables 1 and 3 because they contain items that are the same. The difference between the items on the two bills is 3 colas. The difference in price is £1.50. Therefore 3 colas cost £1.50 and 1 cola costs £1.50 ÷ 3 = 50p. Discuss how £1.50 can be divided by 3. (Change to 150p and divide, or use knowledge that 3 × 50p = £1.50)

- Focus on the bill for Table 1 or 3 and subtract the cost of the colas to arrive at the cost of 3 pizzas and then the cost of 1 pizza. For example, £11 − 50p = £10.50, so the cost of 1 pizza is £10.50 ÷ 3 = £3.50. Discuss how £10.50 can be divided by 3. (Change to 1050p and divide or use trial and improvement.)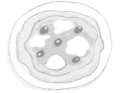

- Focus on the bill for Table 2. Subtract the cost of 2 colas and 1 pizza from the total to arrive at the cost of 2 salads: £8.50 − £4.50 = £4. Therefore the cost of one salad is £2.

- Focus on the bill for Table 4. We now know the cost of all the items and can work out the total bill: (£3.50 × 2) + (£2 × 2) + (50p × 2) = £12

Some children may have worked out the cost of a cola and a pizza by trial and error (trying different prices in the bills for Tables 1 and 3 until the correct totals are arrived at). Point out that this is an acceptable strategy, but not the most efficient, and one that could be very time consuming.

2 Conclude the lesson by pointing out to children that they have been solving problems using known facts to find unknown facts.

Development

Less able: *What is the total bill for all the tables? What was the total cost of the pizzas?*

More able and Average: *If there were 10 people sitting at the 4 tables, what was the mean (average) bill for each person?*

Solutions

PCM 3
The total for Table 4 is £12. (cola is 50p; pizza is £3.50; salad is £2)

Textbook page 12
1 a £10.50   b £3.50
2 £12.50
3 a £4.50   b £4   c £2
4 £12

8 Make a century!

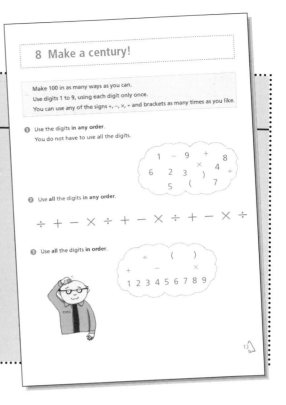

8 Make a century!

Make 100 in as many ways as you can.
Use digits 1 to 9, using each digit only once.
You can use any of the signs +, −, ×, ÷ and brackets as many times as you like.

1 Use the digits **in any order**.
You do not have to use all the digits.

2 Use all the digits **in any order**.

3 Use all the digits **in order**.

13

Minimum prior experience

mental calculations with 2-digit numbers; use of brackets; correct calculator use

Resources

Pupil's Textbook page 13, calculators, digit and sign cards

Key vocabulary

digit, approximate, brackets, operation, calculate, predict, adjust, trial and improvement

What's the problem?

Number investigations that involve reasoning about numbers and operations and require effective calculator use.

Problem solving objectives

- Choose and use appropriate number operations to solve problems, and appropriate ways of calculating.
- Solve mathematical problems or puzzles, recognise and explain patterns and relationships, generalise and predict. Suggest extensions asking 'What if ...?'

Differentiation

More able: Pupil's Textbook page 13, problem 3

Average: Pupil's Textbook page 13, problem 2 (same problem but with fewer conditions)

Less able: Pupil's Textbook page 13, problem 1 (same problem but with limited conditions)

Introducing the problem

Explain to children that in this lesson they will be doing a number puzzle. Go over the general instructions on Textbook page 13 and make clear the specific conditions for the different activities. All groups can use signs and brackets as many times as they wish, and digits can be combined to make numbers, e.g. 12 and 367. Remind children that brackets are used to show which operations should be done first, e.g. in $6 \times (2 + 3)$, the brackets indicate that

2 and 3 must be added before multiplication by 6 (see **Useful mathematical information page 83**). Tell children that they can use a calculator for this investigation if they wish.

Teacher focus for activity

All children: In their recordings, make sure that children are using brackets to indicate, when necessary, which parts of an expression are to be calculated first.

If children are using a simple arithmetic calculator, make sure that they are using it appropriately and not just going through strings of operations from left to right, regardless of brackets (see **Plenary** and **Useful mathematical information page 83**).

As a child works through a trial calculation ask questions such as: *Roughly how much more / less do you need to make 100? What do you need to do to make exactly 100? Can you do that with the digits that are left? How could you adjust your answer so that it makes 100?*

Optional adult input

Work with the Less able group. Encourage children to make use of all the operations.

Plenary

1 Discuss the approaches children used for each investigation (trial and improvement is the most likely approach).

2 For each of problems 2 and 3, invite children to write their results on the board, omitting duplicates.

3 Invite children to say some expressions for problem 1. Use some expressions to reinforce systematic approaches, e.g. if you have found $52 + 48 = 100$ then you can use that as a basis for $58 + 42 = 100$; in the same way, $(51 \times 2) - 6 + 4 = 100$ can be the basis for $(51 \times 2) - 8 + 6$. Write 2 or 3 of the most creative expressions on the board. With the class, go through each calculation as it is presented. If there are any ambiguities as to the order in which the calculations in an expression are carried out, then discuss how the ambiguities can be rectified – possibly with the use of brackets.

4 Discuss with children any mathematical difficulties they may have encountered. These could include:

- The use of brackets
  Write $2 + 3 \times 4$.
  Discuss the ways in which this calculation could be interpreted: 2 add 3, then multiply the answer by 4 (20) or add the result of 3 times 4 to 2 (14). Explain that brackets make it clear how to 'read' a calculation. Brackets always have to be worked out first. So. $(2 + 3) \times 4 = 5 \times 4 = 20$ but $2 + (3 \times 4) = 2 + 12 = 14$

  Demonstrate further using other examples. (See also **Useful mathematical information page 83.**)

- The use of a calculator
  Children may find that using a calculator to do all the calculations in an expression one at a time from left to right results in an incorrect answer. Explain that calculators in primary schools are usually arithmetic (rather than scientific). Arithmetic calculators work through a calculation one at a time in the order in which they are entered. So if $2 + 3 \times 4$ is entered into the calculator in that order, the calculator starts with 2, adds 3 to make 5, then multiplies 5 by 4 to make 20. Brackets cannot be input into arithmetic calculators. Calculators should be used with an understanding of these limitations. (See also **Useful mathematical information page 83.**)

Development

Ask: *Which numbers from 1 to 100 can be made using the digits 1 to 9 once only in any order?* The class could be split into groups with each group investigating a particular range of numbers.

Solutions

1 Here are some solutions. There are many more.
$$62 + 38$$
$$68 + 32$$
$$25 \times 4$$
$$(26 - 1) \times 4$$
$$(51 \times 2) - 6 + 4$$
$$(51 \times 2) - 8 + 6$$

2 Here are some solutions. There may be more.
$$34 + 89 - (2 \times 6) + 1 - 5 - 7 = 100$$
$$348 - 265 + 1 + 7 + 9 = 100$$
$$(38 \div 2) + (7 \times 9) + (4 \times 6) - 1 - 5 = 100$$
Also, any of the results from the More able activity and permissible variations in the order of each.

3 Here are some solutions. There may be more.
$$123 + 45 - 67 + 8 - 9 = 100$$
$$1 + 2 + 3 + 4 + 5 + 6 + 7 + (8 \times 9) = 100$$
$$1 \times (2 + 3) \times (4 \times 5) + 6 - 7 - 8 + 9 = 100$$

9 Dotty polygons

Minimum prior experience

areas of shapes on a grid of centimetre squares

Resources

Pupil's Textbook page 14, PCM 4, large 'write on–wipe off' dotty grid (optional), centimetre square dotty paper, pin boards and elastic bands (optional)

Key vocabulary

area, polygon, perimeter, internal, relationship, formula, general statement, prove

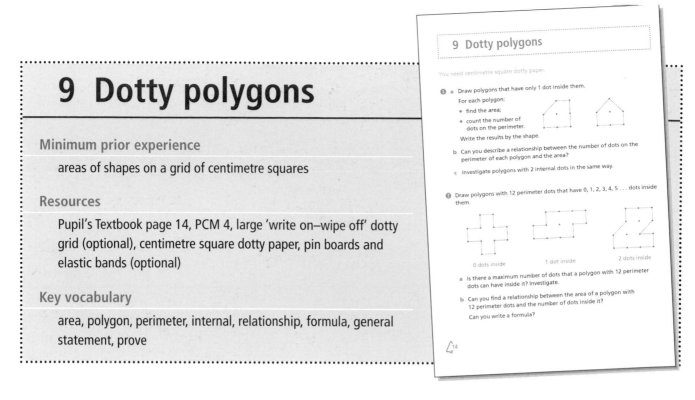

What's the problem?

Investigations into the relationship between the areas of shapes drawn on square dotty paper and the number of internal and perimeter dots. There is the opportunity to express relationships as formulae.

Problem solving objectives

- Explain methods and reasoning, orally and in writing.
- Solve mathematical problems or puzzles, recognise and explain patterns and relationships, generalise and predict. Suggest extensions asking 'What if . . . ?'
- Make and investigate a general statement about familiar numbers or shapes by finding examples that satisfy it.
- Develop from explaining a generalised relationship in words to expressing it in a formula using letters as symbols.

Differentiation

More able: Pupil's Textbook page 14, problem 2

Average: Pupil's Textbook page 14, problem 1 (simpler problem)

Less able: PCM 4 (similar problem to Average, but with step-by-step direction)

Introducing the problem

Revise the meaning of perimeter (distance around, or the boundary of, a 2-D shape) and area (the amount of space inside a 2-D shape).

Briefly look at each problem, ensuring that children understand their particular investigation. Make it clear that the problems involve finding the number of dots on a perimeter, not the perimeter itself. If available, draw children's attention to the pin boards, which they will find useful for creating shapes before drawing them. Remind children that investigations should be recorded in an organised way.

Teacher focus for activity

All children: For children who think they have found a relationship, discuss how many shapes they think they need to investigate before they can confidently make a general statement. Can they ever be sure? Encourage them to test the relationship on 'unusual' examples.

More able: *Can you prove that, for a shape with 12 dots on its perimeter, there either is or is not a maximum number of internal dots?* (See **Useful mathematical information page 83**.)

Optional adult input

Work with the Less able group. Help children to calculate the fractional parts of areas, e.g. by viewing them as half rectangles.

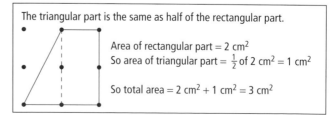

The triangular part is the same as half of the rectangular part.

Area of rectangular part = 2 cm^2
So area of triangular part = $\frac{1}{2}$ of 2 cm^2 = 1 cm^2

So total area = 2 cm^2 + 1 cm^2 = 3 cm^2

Plenary

It would be useful to have on display a large square dotty grid on which shapes can be drawn and wiped off, e.g. on an overhead projector acetate. Otherwise, dots can be drawn on the board for each shape.

1 Focus on PCM 4 and Textbook page 14, problem 1. Invite children from the Average and Less able groups to describe their investigations and findings. Ask them to draw some of their shapes.

Discuss the relationship between the number of dots on the perimeter of a shape and the area. There are 2 ways this can be expressed (one being the converse of the other):

- The number of square centimetres (area) equals half the number of perimeter dots.
- The number of perimeter dots is twice the number of square centimetres (area).

Discuss how each of these could be expressed as a formula: $A = \frac{1}{2}p$ or $2A = p$, where A is the area in square centimetres and p is the number of perimeter dots.

Can we be absolutely certain that this relationship will always apply to all polygons with one dot inside? Discuss. Invite children to draw unusual polygons with one dot inside to test whether the relationship still applies.

2 Focus on Textbook page 14, problem 2. Ask children from the More able group to describe their investigation and findings.

Can children say whether there is a limit to the number of internal dots for a polygon with 12 perimeter dots? Can they explain why (prove it)? Discuss. (See **Useful mathematical information page 83**.)

Discuss the relationship between the area of a polygon with 12 perimeter dots and the number of dots inside it. Children may have found that the number of square centimetres (area) is 5 more than the number of dots inside the polygon (or the converse).

Discuss how this relationship could be expressed as a formula: $A = d + 5$ or $d = A - 5$ where A is the number of square centimetres (area) and d is the number of internal dots.

Development

More able: Children investigate the relationship between area and the number of internal dots in polygons with different numbers of dots on the perimeter.

Average and Less able: Children investigate the relationship between area and the number of perimeter dots in polygons with 2, 3, 4 . . . dots inside them.

Solutions

Textbook page 14

1 a Children's own polygons; area and number of perimeter dots for each polygon.
  b For 1 internal dot, the area in square centimetres is half the number of perimeter dots (or the converse).
  c For 2 internal dots, the area in square centimetres is half the number of perimeter dots plus 1 (or the converse).

2 a No, there is not a maximum number of dots.
  b The area in square centimetres of a polygon with 12 perimeter dots is 5 more than the number of internal dots (or the converse): $A = d + 5$ or $d = A - 5$, where A = area in square centimetres and d = the number of internal dots.

PCM 4

1 a 3 cm^2 b 6 dots
2 a 6 cm^2 b 12 dots
3 a $3\frac{1}{2}$ cm^2 b 7 dots
4 a $5\frac{1}{2}$ cm^2 b 11 dots

The area in square centimetres is half the number of perimeter dots (or the converse).

10 Fractions challenge

What's the problem?

A problem involving reasoning about fractions, finding simple fractions of numbers, equivalent fractions and simple fraction additions.

Problem solving objectives

- Choose and use appropriate number operations to solve problems and appropriate ways of calculating.
- Explain methods and reasoning, orally and in writing.

Differentiation

More able: PCM 5 Fractions challenge 3

Average: PCM 5 Fractions challenge 2 (similar problem, but with simpler fractions)

Less able: PCM 5 Fractions challenge 1 (similar problem, but with simpler and fewer fractions and a clue)

Introducing the problem

Before children start, read through the problems and make sure that they understand what they are being asked to find out. Establish that there are various ways of solving the problems and that you are as interested in **how** they solve them as you are in a correct answer, so they should show their working and thoughts clearly.

Teacher focus for activity

All children: Focus on 'neutral' probing questions such as: *What do you need to do to solve this problem? What do you need to find out first? What have you done so far? What do you need to find out next? How might you be able to find that out?*

For children in the More able or Average groups who are making no headway, use the following clues: *What fraction of the coins did the first 3 children get altogether? So what fraction did the fourth child get?*

More able: If necessary, ask: *What could be the denominator in a fraction that is equivalent to $\frac{1}{3}$? ... $\frac{1}{4}$? ... $\frac{1}{5}$?*

Average and Less able: You may need to establish that fractions need to be converted to equivalent fractions with a common denominator before they can be added. A fraction 'wall' showing quarters, thirds, sixths and twelfths would be helpful.

Optional adult input

Work with the Less able group on equivalent fractions, using a fraction wall and making equivalent fraction patterns such as $\frac{1}{3}, \frac{2}{6}, \frac{3}{9}, \frac{4}{12} \ldots$

$\frac{1}{3}$		$\frac{1}{3}$		$\frac{1}{3}$	
$\frac{1}{6}$	$\frac{1}{6}$	$\frac{1}{6}$	$\frac{1}{6}$	$\frac{1}{6}$	$\frac{1}{6}$

Plenary

Display an enlarged version of Fractions challenge 2.

1 Explain to children that you are going to focus on problem 2, but that the other problems can be dealt with in a similar way. Invite children to explain how the problem can be solved, encouraging children from all groups to contribute. Make sure that the methods are understood. These are likely to be along the following lines:

- Write an expression to find the total of the fractions received by Mindy, Mandy and Mog:
$\frac{1}{4} + \frac{1}{6} + \frac{1}{12}$

- Use equivalent fractions to express the statement with common denominators and add them up:
$\frac{1}{4} + \frac{1}{6} + \frac{1}{12} = \frac{3}{12} + \frac{2}{12} + \frac{1}{12} = \frac{6}{12}$ (or $\frac{1}{2}$)

- Work out the fraction that was received by Meg:
$\frac{12}{12} - \frac{6}{12} = \frac{6}{12}$ (or $\frac{1}{2}$)

- Equate Meg's fraction with the number of coins she got:
$\frac{6}{12}$ = 6 coins. So $\frac{1}{12}$ = 1 coin

- Calculate Mog's amount:
Mog received $\frac{1}{12}$ = 1 coin

2 *How can we check the answer?* Discuss and use the children's suggestions. A likely suggestion is as follows:

- Work out how many coins the other children received, knowing that $\frac{1}{12}$ = 1 coin.

- Find the total number of coins by adding.

- Work through the problem again, knowing the total number of coins.

3 Establish the correct answers for each of the other problems.

4 Discuss any difficulties that children had with the mathematics involved. These might include:

- Adding fractions.
Establish that fractions need to be converted to equivalent fractions with the same denominator before they can be added. For fractions such as $\frac{1}{4}$, $\frac{1}{6}$ and $\frac{1}{12}$ (Fractions challenge 2), a fraction wall could be used to change the fractions to twelfths:

For sets of fractions such as $\frac{1}{3}$, $\frac{1}{4}$ and $\frac{1}{5}$ (Fractions challenge 3), the lowest common multiple of all the denominators needs to be found. (For a full explanation, see **Useful mathematical information pages 83–84**.)

- Finding the fraction that the last child (Seth, Meg or Jo) received.
Help children to understand that the whole pot is 1 and that 1 can be represented by any fraction in which the numerator and denominator are the same, for example, $\frac{3}{3}$, $\frac{4}{4}$, $\frac{5}{5}$, $\frac{20}{20}$. So if $\frac{1}{3}$ of the pot is used then the fraction of the pot remaining is $\frac{3}{3} - \frac{1}{3} = \frac{2}{3}$

Development

Children make up similar problems at their level – perhaps using only 2 fractions. They must be able to work out the solution themselves.

Solutions

Fractions challenge 1
Jill got 2 coins.

Fractions challenge 2
Mog got 1 coin.

Fractions challenge 3
Sandy got 15 coins.

1 whole											
$\frac{1}{4}$			$\frac{1}{4}$			$\frac{1}{4}$			$\frac{1}{4}$		
$\frac{1}{6}$		$\frac{1}{6}$		$\frac{1}{6}$		$\frac{1}{6}$		$\frac{1}{6}$		$\frac{1}{6}$	
$\frac{1}{12}$	$\frac{1}{12}$	$\frac{1}{12}$	$\frac{1}{12}$	$\frac{1}{12}$	$\frac{1}{12}$	$\frac{1}{12}$	$\frac{1}{12}$	$\frac{1}{12}$	$\frac{1}{12}$	$\frac{1}{12}$	$\frac{1}{12}$

11 Stamps

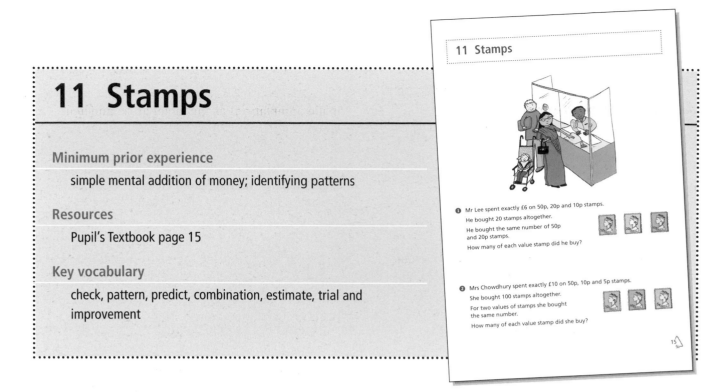

11 Stamps

❶ Mr Lee spent exactly £6 on 50p, 20p and 10p stamps.
He bought 20 stamps altogether.
He bought the same number of 50p and 20p stamps.
How many of each value stamp did he buy?

❷ Mrs Chowdhury spent exactly £10 on 50p, 10p and 5p stamps.
She bought 100 stamps altogether.
For two values of stamps she bought the same number.
How many of each value stamp did she buy?

15

Minimum prior experience

simple mental addition of money; identifying patterns

Resources

Pupil's Textbook page 15

Key vocabulary

check, pattern, predict, combination, estimate, trial and improvement

What's the problem?

A problem about the purchase of postage stamps involving mental addition of money, identifying patterns to make predictions and reasoning about numbers.

Problem solving objectives

- Solve mathematical problems or puzzles, recognise and explain patterns and relationships, generalise and predict. Suggest extensions asking 'What if . . . ?'
- Identify and use appropriate operations to solve word problems involving numbers and quantities based on 'real life', money or measures using one or more steps.
  Explain methods and reasoning.

Differentiation

More able: Pupil's Textbook page 15, problem 2

Average: Pupil's Textbook page 15, problem 2 (same problem, but with discretionary guidance about organising results)

Less able: Pupil's Textbook page 15, problem 1 (similar problem, but with more restricted possibilities and less demanding numbers)

Introducing the problem

Read through the problems with children. Ensure that they understand the data and the question by asking, e.g. *How much did Mrs Chowdhury spend on stamps? How many stamps did Mr Lee buy? What else are you told? What have you got to find out?*

Invite children to suggest ways in which they might tackle their problem, but give no indication of the relative value of one approach over another.

Remind children that they can choose their own method of recording and that you will be interested in the different ways the problems are tackled.

Teacher focus for activity

All children: Initially ask children to explain how they intend to tackle the problem. Children may start by randomly trying out different combinations of stamps. If they continue to do so, point out that this way of working makes it difficult to keep track of tried combinations. Ask them to suggest a more ordered way of trying different combinations. If necessary, the use of a table could be suggested.

For those who find a solution, ask: *Is this the only solution?*

Less able: If, after a while, children do not progress beyond random trials, show them how to systematically investigate possible combinations of 20 stamps using a table. Encourage them to look for patterns to help them continue the table.

50p	20p	10p	value
1	1	18	£2.50
2	2	16	£3.00
3	3	14	£3.50

Optional adult input

Work with the More able group, encouraging children to record their investigations clearly, e.g. in tabular form.

Plenary

1   Ask children from each group to explain how they approached their problem. Make sure that the rest of the class understand the explanations and encourage them to ask questions and make comments and suggestions. During the course of the explanations discuss the merits of systematic investigations over more random approaches. Establish that systematic approaches are more efficient, making it easier to check combinations of stamps that have already been considered. Patterns emerge more clearly in a systematic approach, enabling predictions to be made and maybe saving unnecessary calculations.

A likely systematic approach to problem 2 (which may emerge during discussions or which you could otherwise introduce) is to consider all combinations of 100 stamps and their values when there is an equal number of:

50p and 10p stamps

50p	10p	5p	value
1	1	98	£5.50
2	2	96	£6.00
3	3	94	£6.50
4			

50p and 5p stamps

50p	10p	5p	value
1	1	98	£10.35
2	2	96	£10.70
3	3	94	£11.05
4			

10p and 5p stamps

50p	10p	5p	value
1	1	98	£49.15
2	2	96	£48.30
3	3	94	£47.45
4			

2   Draw each table on the board and invite children to help you complete each one. Encourage them to make observations as the tables are completed. Patterns and impossibilities should become apparent, e.g.

- In the first table, continuing the £5.50, £6.00, £6.50 pattern, it becomes clear that £10 is achieved in the 10th row (10 × 50p, 10 × 10p, 80 × 5p).

- In the second table, continuing the £10.35, £10.70, £11.05 pattern (increasing in steps of 35p), it becomes clear that £10 is impossible to achieve.

- The third table is not so straightforward, but children might observe that the value is reduced by 85p in each row and that there are few rows which result in a whole number of pounds. Establish that if £10 can be achieved it will be much further down in the table. Invite children to suggest combinations to try. It should emerge that £10 is impossible to achieve. (See **Useful mathematical information page 84** for a further analysis of this table.)

Development

What if there are twice as many stamps of one value as another?

Solutions

1   8 fifty pence stamps, 8 twenty pence stamps and 4 ten pence stamps

2   10 fifty pence stamps, 10 ten pence stamps and 80 five pence stamps

12 Problems at work

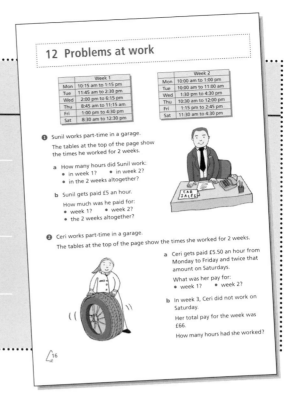

12 Problems at work

Week 1	
Mon	10:15 am to 1:15 pm
Tue	11:45 am to 2:30 pm
Wed	2:00 pm to 6:15 pm
Thu	8:45 am to 11:15 am
Fri	1:00 pm to 4:30 pm
Sat	8:30 am to 12:30 pm

Week 2	
Mon	10:00 am to 1:00 pm
Tue	10:00 am to 11:00 am
Wed	1:30 pm to 4:30 pm
Thu	10:30 am to 12:00 pm
Fri	1:15 pm to 2:45 pm
Sat	11:30 am to 4:30 pm

❶ Sunil works part-time in a garage.
The tables at the top of the page show
the times he worked for 2 weeks.

a How many hours did Sunil work:
  • in week 1?   • in week 2?
  • in the 2 weeks altogether?

b Sunil gets paid £5 an hour.
  How much was he paid for:
  • week 1?   • week 2?
  • the 2 weeks altogether?

❷ Ceri works part-time in a garage.
The tables at the top of the page show the times she worked for 2 weeks.

a Ceri gets paid £5.50 an hour from
Monday to Friday and twice that
amount on Saturdays.
What was her pay for:
  • week 1?   • week 2?

b In week 3, Ceri did not work on
Saturday.
Her total pay for the week was
£66.
How many hours had she worked?

16

What's the problem?

'Real-life' multi-step problems based on hourly rates of pay at work and weekly wages. They involve choosing and using appropriate number operations, calculating with time and money and checking results of calculations.

Problem solving objectives

- Choose and use appropriate number operations to solve problems and appropriate ways of calculating.

- Identify and use appropriate operations to solve word problems involving numbers and quantities based on 'real life', money or measures, using one or more steps.
  Explain methods and reasoning.

Differentiation

More able: Pupil's Textbook page 17 (problem 3)

Average: Pupil's Textbook page 16, problem 2 (similar problem, but with less demanding numbers and greater structure)

Less able: Pupil's Textbook page 16, problem 1 (similar problem, but with less demanding numbers and questions)

Introducing the problem

Before children start, give them a few minutes to read through the problems and to ask questions about anything that is not clear. To avoid confusion, explain that, although the time sheets are the same for each

problem, the rates of pay in each problem are different, because the people do different jobs.

Teacher focus for activity

All children: Initially ask questions such as: *What do you need to find out? How will you do that? What information do you have? What sort of calculation will you need to do?*

As children work, ask them to talk you through what they have done so far and what they will do next.

Encourage children to estimate answers before they start on a calculation, e.g. by scanning a time sheet and estimating the total time worked; by approximating the total pay for the week, once the total time and hourly rate is known.

Encourage children to devise a method of checking each answer, e.g. adding times in a different order; using a division to check a multiplication.

Optional adult input

Work with the Less able group. Help children to calculate hours worked each day by counting on from the start time to the finish time.

❸ Jake works part-time in a garage.
The tables on page 16 show the times he worked for 2 weeks.

a Jake gets paid a fixed hourly rate.
For week 1 his total pay was £90.
What was Jake's pay for week 2?

b For week 3, Jake's pay was £54.
How many hours had he worked?

Plenary

1 Explain that you are going to focus on the first part of problem 3, but that information found out by the Average and Less able groups will help to solve it.

Ask: *What are we asked to find out?* (Jake's pay at the end of week 2) *What information are we given?* (Jake's pay at the end of week 1) *What do we need to know before we can work out Jake's pay for week 2?* (the number of hours he worked in week 2 and his rate of pay)

2 Discuss with children what they would like to calculate first. They might want to work out the number of hours he worked in week 2 first or his rate of pay. Try whichever they suggest. Discuss whether it would matter which part was worked out first.

● Calculating the number of hours worked in week 2
Invite children to give the number of hours Jake worked in week 2 and to explain how they worked it out.

Establish that Jake worked for 15 hours in week 2.

● Calculating the rate of pay
Ask children to suggest how Jake's rate of pay could be calculated. Establish that we know how much he was paid for week 1. If we work out how many hours he worked in week 1 we could calculate what he is paid for each hour.

Invite children to give the number of hours Jake worked in week 1. You could check the answers with the class by getting them to calculate the

hours for each day, one at a time and then finding the total.

Establish that in week 1, Jake worked for 20 hours and was paid £90.

How can we work out his hourly rate of pay? Discuss children's suggestions. These could include trial and improvement methods, e.g. estimating the rate of pay to be, say, £4, then multiplying by 20 (£4 × 20 = £80) and then gradually adjusting until the estimated amount multiplied by 20 gives £90. Some children may notice that £90 divided by 20 is '£4$\frac{1}{2}$'.

Establish that the rate of pay is £4.50

3 *We now know that Jake worked for 15 hours in week 2 and that his hourly rate of pay is £4.50.*

Discuss how Jake's pay for week 2 can now be worked out (£4.50 × 15).

Ask children to suggest ways in which this could be calculated. Methods could include mental strategies such as multiplying the £4 by 15 (£60) and the 50p by 15 (£7.50) and adding the two results (£67.50), or multiplying £4.50 by 10 (£45) and halving £45 to find 5 times £4.50 (£22.50), then adding the results (£45 + £22.50 = £67.50)

Establish that in week 2, Jake's pay was £67.50.

Development

If 20% of each person's pay is deducted for tax and National Insurance, what is each person's 'take home' pay for each week?

Solutions

1 a 20 hours; 15 hours; 35 hours
  b £100; £75; £175

2 a £132; £110   **b** 12 hours

3 a £67.50   **b** 12 hours

13 How old?

Minimum prior experience

units of time (second, minute, hour, day, week, month, year); simple addition and multiplication

Resources

Pupil's Textbook page 18, calendars, calculators (discretionary)

Key vocabulary

second, minute, hour, day, week, month, year, leap year, convert

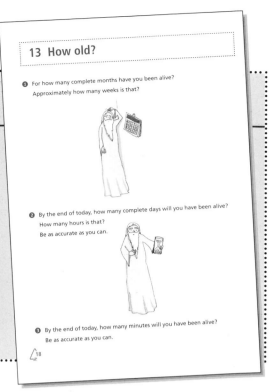

13 How old?

❶ For how many complete months have you been alive?
Approximately how many weeks is that?

❷ By the end of today, how many complete days will you have been alive?
How many hours is that?
Be as accurate as you can.

❸ By the end of today, how many minutes will you have been alive?
Be as accurate as you can.

18

What's the problem?

Children work out how long they have been alive. The problems involve conversion from one unit of time to another, addition and multiplication and can involve large numbers and an understanding of leap years.

Problem solving objectives

- Choose and use appropriate number operations to solve problems and appropriate ways of calculating.
- Identify and use appropriate operations to solve word problems involving numbers and quantities based on 'real life', money or measures, using one or more steps.
  Explain methods and reasoning.

Differentiation

More able: Pupil's Textbook page 18, problem 3 (calculating in minutes)

Average: Pupil's Textbook page 18, problem 2 (similar problem, but calculating in hours)

Less able: Pupil's Textbook page 18, problem 1 (similar problem, but calculating in months, then weeks)

Introducing the problem

Invite children to say how old they are. Each time, ask if it would be possible to give their age more accurately. What units would they use?

Explain that in this lesson they are going to work out how old they are as exactly as they can. Remind them to record their working clearly. Children should then tackle the problem straight away.

Teacher focus for activity

Average and More able: Encourage children to be as exact as they can be. Unless children know the exact time of their birth, discuss with them what they will count it as for this problem, e.g. 12 midnight after the birth.

Where necessary, remind children that there are not exactly 4 weeks (28 days) in each month.

Less able: For children who are making no headway, ask leading questions such as: *How many months make a year? How many years have you been alive? How could you work out how many months that is? Have you been alive longer than that? How much longer? How could we find out?*

Children may find it helpful to use a calendar to count on in months.

Optional adult input

Work with the More able group, checking that children's calculations are correct and asking them to explain what they have done so far.

Plenary

1   Invite children from each group to say how old they are as exactly as they can.

   Ask individuals to explain how they arrived at their answer. Help the rest of the class to understand the explanations and encourage them to ask questions.

   After each answer and explanation, discuss if the answer could have been more exact (but still using the same unit).

Make sure that the following ways of being more exact are included in the discussions:

- working from the exact time of birth (problem 3);

- taking leap years into account (problems 2 and 3).

2 Ask children to explain how they think leap years could be taken into account.
Establish that:

- There are 366 days in a leap year (the extra day coming at the end of February).

- Leap years occur every fourth year.

Discuss how leap years can be identified (they are exactly divisible by 4 – for exceptions to this rule see **Useful mathematical information pages 84–85**). Ask children to identify leap years that have occurred during their life. Discuss how children could use this knowledge to make their answers more exact.

3 Ask children to give examples of any mathematics that they had difficulty with and discuss them. These might include:

- Reading large numbers
Remind children that it can be helpful to arrange the digits of large numbers in blocks of three from the right. Write some examples of large numbers on the board. Ask individuals to arrange the digits and then ask children to read the numbers as you point to each block of digits in turn (from the left).

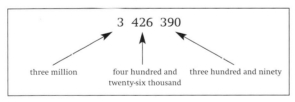

3 426 390

three million   four hundred and   three hundred and ninety
              twenty-six thousand

- Multiplication by 12, 24 or 60
Ask children to give examples of where they had to multiply by 12, 24 or 60.
Discuss different methods that could be used, e.g.

  To multiply by 12:
  multiply the number by 10, then by 2, then add the answers;
  multiply by 6 and double;
  use a written multiplication method.

  To multiply by 24:
  multiply the number by 20, then by 4, then add the answers;
  multiply by 6 then double and double again;
  use a written multiplication method.

  To multiply by 60:
  multiply by 6, then multiply the answer by 10 (or vice versa).

(For a written 'grid' method of multiplication see **Useful mathematical information page 83**.)

Development

Children improve the accuracy of their answers, e.g. by including leap years if they had not done so before, or by finding out their exact time of birth and modifying their answers. Children could also convert their answers to the next smaller unit.

Solutions

These will vary but will be at least:
For 10 year-olds:
120 months (10 × 12 months);
480 weeks (120 × 4 weeks);
3650 days (10 × 365 days);
87 600 hours (3650 × 24 hours);
5 256 000 minutes (87 600 × 60 minutes)

For 11 year-olds:
132 months (11 × 12 months);
528 weeks (132 × 4 weeks);
4015 days (11 × 365 days);
96 360 hours (4015 × 24 hours);
5 781 600 minutes (96 360 × 60 minutes)

14 Personal weights

Minimum prior experience

addition and subtraction of 2- and 3-digit numbers;
the inverse relationship between addition and subtraction

Resources

Pupil's Textbook page 19, PCM 6, enlarged copy of PCM 6
Personal weights 2

Key vocabulary

mass, weight, scales, kilogram, if . . . then, sum, total, difference,
trial and improvement

14 Personal weights

The Hoskins family live on a farm.
Mr Hoskins knows that he weighs 80 kg.
The rest of the family want to know what they weigh.

The only scales they have are old ones used for weighing sheep.
The scales won't weigh anything under 100 kg.
So they get on the scales 2 at a time.

Mr Hoskins — 80 kg

Mr and Mrs Hoskins together — 155 kg

Mrs Hoskins and her son Mat together — 149 kg

Mat and his sister Sally together — 142 kg

What does each member of the family weigh?

Remember! You already know what Mr Hoskins weighs.

What's the problem?

An essentially algebraic problem in the context of weight. Children reason about known data to find unknown data.

Problem solving objectives:

- Choose and use appropriate number operations to solve problems, and appropriate ways of calculating.

- Solve mathematical problems or puzzles, recognise and explain patterns and relationships, generalise and predict. Suggest extensions asking 'What if . . . ?'

- Identify and use appropriate operations to solve word problems involving numbers and quantities based on 'real life', money or measures, using one or more steps.
  Explain methods and reasoning.

Differentiation

More able: PCM 6 Personal weights 2

Average: PCM 6 Personal weights 1 (similar problem, but with fewer pieces of information to manipulate)

Less able: Pupil's Textbook page 19 (similar problem, but with one weight given)

Introducing the problem

Set the general scene of a family wanting to weigh themselves, having scales that will only weigh things over 100 kilograms, and deciding to weigh themselves two at a time. Explain to children that they should show all their working as you are as interested in

how they solve their problem as you are in the actual answer.

Teacher focus for activity

More able and Average:
Children may find it helpful to draw diagrams or pictures to represent pairs of people on the scales and the scale reading.

Whose weight (mass) do you think you could find out first? Why? How will you do it? Whose weight (mass) could you find then? How?

Mrs — 155 kg — Mr

(See **Useful mathematical information page 85** for an explanation of the difference between mass and weight.)

Less able: Only if children are finding it difficult to get started, ask questions such as: *How much does Mr. Hoskins weigh? How much do Mr and Mrs Hoskins weigh altogether? So how could you find out what Mrs Hoskins weighs?*

Children who solve the problem can work out the combined weights of various other pairs in the family such as Mr Hoskins and Mat; Mrs Hoskins and Sally.

Optional adult input

Work with the Less able group, helping children to decide how to solve the calculations involved.

Plenary

1 Display an enlarged version of PCM 6 Personal weights 2.
Explain that everyone has been working towards the same answers but starting with slightly different information.
Invite children from the More able and Average groups to say which part of the problem they tackled first.
Why did you start there? How did you work that out?

2 Similarly, ask different children to explain how they tackled the subsequent parts of the problem. Ensure that the Less able group is involved, especially once Mr Hoskins's weight has been calculated.

Here is one method of solving the problem:

- Mrs Hoskins and Mat weigh 147 kg. Mr Hoskins and Mat weigh 152 kg.
Because Mat is included in both weights, the difference in the 2 weights must be accounted for by the difference in weight between Mr and Mrs Hoskins.
The difference in the weights is
152 kg − 147 kg = 5 kg.
So Mr Hoskins is 5 kg heavier than Mrs Hoskins.

- Mr and Mrs Hoskins together weigh 155 kg. The difference in their weights is 5 kg.
We need to find two weights with a total of 155 kg and a difference of 5 kg.
We could do this by trial and improvement, e.g. by guessing 70 kg and 85 kg (total: 155 kg; difference: 15 kg) and gradually increasing one weight and reducing the other by the same amount until a difference of 5 kg is arrived at:

Mrs	Mr
70 kg	85 kg (15 kg difference)
73 kg	82 kg (9 kg ")
75 kg	80 kg (5 kg ")

Or we could be more systematic, by dividing 155 kg into two equal halves of 77.5 kg and adjusting from there until there is a difference of 5 kg:

Mrs	Mr
77.5 kg	77.5 kg (0 kg difference)
77 kg	78 kg (1 kg ")
76 kg	79 kg (3 kg ")
75 kg	80 kg (5 kg ")

Or we could reason:
Mr and Mrs Hoskins weigh 155 kg:
Mr + Mrs = 155 kg
Mrs Hoskins is 5 kg lighter than Mr Hoskins, so 2 lots of Mrs Hoskins's weight must be 5 kg less than 155 kg: Mrs + Mrs = 150 kg
Mrs Hoskins must weigh half of 150 kg, which is 75 kg.
Mr Hoskins is 5 kg heavier than Mrs Hoskins, so he weighs 75 kg + 5 kg = 80 kg

- Knowing that Mrs Hoskins weighs 75 kg and Mr Hoskins weighs 80 kg, we can now substitute either weight in one of the combined weights including Mat, e.g.
We know that Mrs Hoskins and Mat together weigh 147 kg, and Mrs Hoskins weighs 75 kg, so Mat must weigh 147 kg − 75 kg = 72 kg

- We know that Mat and Sally together weigh 142 kg and that Mat weighs 72 kg, so Sally must weigh 142 kg − 72 kg = 70 kg

(See **Useful mathematical information page 85** for another method.)

Development

Ask: *What if the scales only registered weights over 200 kg, how could the family find out their weights?*

Solutions

Mr Hoskins: 80 kg; Mrs Hoskins: 75 kg; Mat: 72 kg; Sally: 70 kg

15 Road signs

15 Road signs

A new law has gone out to all villages and towns.

The law says that wherever 2 roads intersect there must be a road sign.

Mapledon has 3 roads that all intersect.

It will need 3 road signs.

Mapledon village

3 roads   3 signs

① What is the maximum number of signs needed in a village with:
  • 2 roads?   • 3 roads?   • 4 roads?   • 5 roads?

Draw diagrams to help you.

3 roads need 3 signs

Copy and complete this table.

roads	1	2	3	4	5	6
signs						

② Can you predict the maximum number of signs needed for:
  • 7 roads?   • 8 roads?   • 9 roads?

20

Minimum prior experience

identifying and continuing number patterns

Resources

Pupil's Textbook pages 20 and 21

Key vocabulary

pattern, relationship, sequence, formula, rule, predict, systematic, triangular number, intersect

What's the problem?

An algebraic investigation in which children identify and explain number patterns and relationships, and generalise in words and perhaps with a formula.

Problem solving objectives

• Explain methods and reasoning, orally and in writing.

• Solve mathematical problems or puzzles, recognise and explain patterns and relationships, generalise and predict. Suggest extensions asking 'What if . . . ?'

• Make and investigate a general statement about familiar numbers or shapes by finding examples that satisfy it.

Differentiation

More able: Pupil's Textbook page 21, question 4. An extra challenge is also provided.

Average: Pupil's Textbook page 21, question 3 (same problem, but with less demanding predictions and describing relationships in words only)

Less able: Pupil's Textbook page 20, questions 1 and 2 (same problem, but with a more guided approach)

Introducing the problem

Go over the information at the top of Textbook page 20. Make sure children understand the meaning of 'intersect'. Emphasise that they will be investigating the **maximum** number of road signs needed in each town, e.g. for 3 roads, the arrangement giving the maximum number is

rather than

Explain that they should record their investigation and what they find out.

Teacher focus for activity

More able and Average: For any pattern to appear, children will need to work systematically, investigating 1, 2, 3, 4 . . . roads in turn. For children who appear not to be working systematically, ask, e.g. *How many roads are you investigating now? Why that number of roads? Have you investigated fewer roads? How many roads are you going to investigate next? Why that number?*

When children have generated a set of ordered results for numbers of signs, ask them to describe any patterns. They may recognise the numbers as triangular numbers (see **Useful mathematical information pages 82–83**).

Children trying to find a formula will probably find it helpful to enter their data into a table.

Less able: Help children to construct diagrams, e.g. building on a 3-road diagram: *For the maximum number of signs, how many roads will the 4th road need to cross?* (all 3)

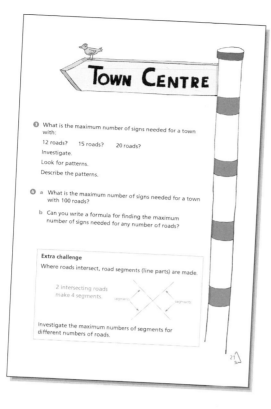

Optional adult input

Work with the Average group. Ask children to predict the number of signs for the number of roads they are investigating and to justify their prediction.

Plenary

1 Invite children to explain what they have found.

Establish that the most fruitful way of investigating is systematically: in this case, finding out the maximum number of signs needed for 1, 2, 3, 4, 5 ... roads.

2 For more than 5 roads, drawing diagrams becomes complicated. Can children see a pattern that will enable them to predict the next few numbers?

Establish that the sequence of numbers of signs seems to be made by increasing the difference between consecutive numbers by 1 each time:

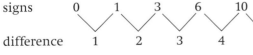

Does anyone recognise this pattern of numbers?

Establish that the numbers are the triangular numbers (see **Useful mathematical information pages 82–83**).

3 *Can you predict the maximum number signs needed for 6, 7, 8 ... 15 roads?* (15, 21, 28, 36, 45, 55, 66, 78, 91, 105)
What about 100 roads? Establish that you could extend the pattern of numbers, but this would take a long time. *We need to find a relationship between the number of roads and the number of signs.*

If any children managed to do this, ask them to explain the relationship.

It would be helpful to tabulate the number of roads and the number of signs. **Draw this table:**

roads	1	2	3	4	5	6	7	8
signs	0	1	3	6	10	15	21	28

If no one can explain the relationship, you could suggest that children focus on the rotated 'L' shapes in the table.

2	3
1	3

4	5
6	10

They may notice that the bottom number is equal to half the product of the upper numbers.

Can children use this relationship to make a general statement and a formula?
One possibility is:

To find the number of signs, multiply the number of roads by one less than the number of roads and divide by two.

As a formula:

$s = r \times (r - 1) \div 2$, where s is the maximum number of signs and r is the number of roads.

Development

Ask: *What if signs are only required where roads intersect at right angles, or 60°?*

Solutions

1

roads	1	2	3	4	5	6
signs	0	1	3	6	10	15

2 7 roads: 21 signs; 8 roads: 28 signs; 9 roads: 36 signs

3 12 roads: 66 signs; 15 roads: 105 signs; 20 roads: 190 signs

The difference between consecutive numbers of signs increases by 1 each time. (The numbers make the sequence of triangular numbers.)

4 a 4950
  b $s = r \times (r - 1) \div 2$ where s is the maximum number of signs and r is the number of roads
  Extra challenge: square numbers are generated

16 Calculation investigation

Minimum prior experience

standard written methods for the 4 operations; place value

Resources

Pupil's Textbook pages 22 and 23, calculators (discretionary)

Key vocabulary

predict, digit, greater than (>), less than (<), calculation, sum, product, difference, quotient, ascending order, general statement, formula

What's the problem?

Investigating the arrangements of digits in standard written algorithms that will result in the largest and smallest answers. Investigations involve reasoning about numbers, place value, an understanding of number operations and making generalisations. There are opportunities to use letter symbols to represent unknown variables.

Problem solving objectives

- Explain methods and reasoning, orally and in writing.
- Solve mathematical problems or puzzles, recognise and explain patterns and relationships, generalise and predict. Suggest extensions asking 'What if . . . ?'
- Make and investigate a general statement about familiar numbers or shapes by finding examples that satisfy it.
- Develop from explaining a generalised relationship in words to expressing it in a formula using letters as symbols.

Differentiation

More able: Pupil's Textbook page 23, questions 7 and 8

Average: Pupil's Textbook page 23, questions 3 to 6 (similar problems, but generalising after trying given numbers)

Less able: Pupil's Textbook page 22, questions 1 and 2 (similar problems, but positioning given numbers in a range of operations)

Introducing the problem

Write the digits 4, 6 and 9 and an empty-box multiplication as shown.

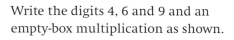
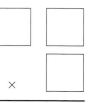

Discuss ways of arranging the digits in the boxes to make the largest and smallest products (64×9 and 69×4).

Explain that children will be investigating the arrangements of digits in other calculations to produce the largest and smallest answers.

Teacher focus for activity

All children: Encourage reasoning about the positioning of digits: *Why have you put that digit there? Where is the best place to put the largest/smallest digit? Why? Would the answer be larger or smaller if you swapped those digits around?*

More able: You may need to suggest that children try examples with actual digits before making generalisations with letters.

Average: When children are working out a rule for the arrangement of digits, they may find it helpful to use letters to represent numbers.

Less able: Can children think of a rule for arranging the digits in each calculation? (e.g. With addition, putting the largest digits in the hundreds column.)

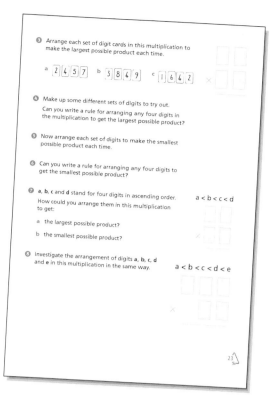

3 Arrange each set of digit cards in this multiplication to make the largest possible product each time.

a ⟨2⟩⟨4⟩⟨5⟩⟨7⟩ b ⟨3⟩⟨8⟩⟨4⟩⟨9⟩ c ⟨1⟩⟨6⟩⟨4⟩⟨2⟩ ×

4 Make up some different sets of digits to try out.

Can you write a rule for arranging any four digits in the multiplication to get the largest possible product?

5 Now arrange each set of digits to make the smallest possible product each time.

6 Can you write a rule for arranging any four digits to get the smallest possible product?

7 a, b, c and d stand for four digits in ascending order. How could you arrange them in this multiplication to get:

a < b < c < d

a the largest possible product?

b the smallest possible product?

8 Investigate the arrangement of digits a, b, c, d and e in this multiplication in the same way.

a < b < c < d < e

Optional adult input

Work with the Less able group, asking children to explain their reasons for the positioning of various digits.

Plenary

1 Write question 1d on the board.

Invite children to write the digits in the boxes to obtain the largest product. Establish that the arrangement of digits that produces the largest product is 432 × 5.

Can children think of a general rule for positioning any set of digits in this algorithm? (e.g. Multiply by the largest digit. Put the next largest digit in the hundreds position, the next in the tens and the smallest in the units position.)

Can they express this rule using the letters a, b, c and d to stand for digits in ascending order?

```
    c  b  a
×         d
─────────────
```

2 Write question 3a on the board.
Establish that the arrangement of digits that produces the largest product is 72 × 54 or 54 × 72.

Can children think of a general rule for arranging the digits? (e.g. Pair the largest digit with the smallest, putting the larger digit in the tens. Pair the second largest digit with the second smallest digit, putting the larger digit in the tens.)

Can they express this using the letters a, b, c and d to represent the digits in ascending order?

```
    c  b              d  a
×   d  a          ×   c  b
─────────        ─────────
```

3 Conclude by reminding children that they have been investigating calculations and making general statements about them.

Development

Children investigate other operations and make generalisations about largest and smallest answers.

Solutions

(other equivalent solutions are possible)

1 a 752 + 631 = 1383   **b** 93 + 82 + 41 = 216
  c 765 − 123 = 642   **d** 432 × 5 = 2160
  e 654 ÷ 3 = 218   **f** 32 × 41 = 1312
2 a 136 + 257 = 393   **b** 14 + 28 + 39 = 81
  c 612 − 573 = 39   **d** 345 × 2 = 690
  e 345 ÷ 6 = 57 r 3 or 57.5
  f 13 × 24 = 312

3 a 54 × 72 = 3888   **b** 84 × 93 = 7812
  c 42 × 61 = 2562
  (or reversing the order of multiplication)
4 Children's own examples followed by a rule: Pair the largest digit with the smallest, putting the larger digit in the tens. Pair the second largest digit with the second smallest digit, putting the larger digit in the tens.
5 a 25 × 47 = 1175   **b** 38 × 49 = 1862
  c 14 × 26 = 364
  (or reversing the order of multiplication)
6 Pair the smallest digit with the second largest, putting the smaller digit in the tens. Pair the second smallest digit with the largest digit, putting the smaller digit in the tens.

7 a
```
    c  b    or    d  a
×   d  a      ×   c  b
```
b
```
    a  c    or    b  d
×   b  d      ×   a  c
```

8
```
    d  c  a   (largest       a  c  e   (smallest
×      e  b   product)   ×      b  d   product)
```

17 School disco

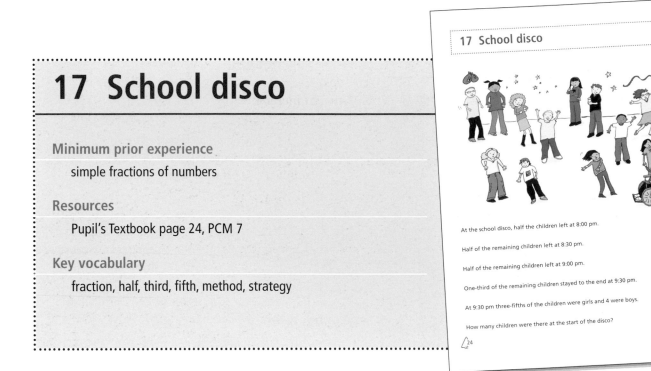

17 School disco

At the school disco, half the children left at 8:00 pm.

Half of the remaining children left at 8:30 pm.

Half of the remaining children left at 9:00 pm.

One-third of the remaining children stayed to the end at 9:30 pm.

At 9:30 pm three-fifths of the children were girls and 4 were boys.

How many children were there at the start of the disco?

24

Minimum prior experience

simple fractions of numbers

Resources

Pupil's Textbook page 24, PCM 7

Key vocabulary

fraction, half, third, fifth, method, strategy

What's the problem?

A problem in a 'real-life' context that involves an understanding of the relationships between fractions and division, and between division and multiplication.

Problem solving objectives

- Choose and use appropriate number operations to solve problems and appropriate ways of calculating.
- Identify and use appropriate operations to solve word problems involving numbers and quantities based on 'real life', money or measures, using one or more steps.
  Explain methods and reasoning.

Differentiation

More able: Pupil's Textbook page 24

Average: PCM 7 School disco 2 (same problem, but with less data to manipulate)

Less able: PCM 7 School disco 1 (same problem, but with even less data to manipulate)

Introducing the problem

Allow children time to read through the problems and ask questions before they start. Explain that there is more than one way to solve these problems and that you are as interested in **how** they solve the problems as you are in a correct answer, so they should show their working and thoughts as they work on the problem.

Teacher focus for activity

If necessary, ask questions that direct children towards the end of the problem and the idea of working backwards, e.g.

More able: *At 9:30, what fraction of the children were boys?* (two fifths) *And how many boys were there?* (4) *So how many children make one fifth?* (2) *So how many children were there altogether at the end?* (10)

Average: *How many children were there at 9:30?* (10) *What fraction of the children who remained after 9:00 are the 10 children?* (one third) *So how many children remained after 9:00?* (30)

Less able: *How many children were left at the end?* (30) *So how many children were there just before 9:00?* (60)

Some children may find it helpful to draw a shape to represent the children at the start of the disco and then to cross out fractions of the shape to represent those who leave at each stage.

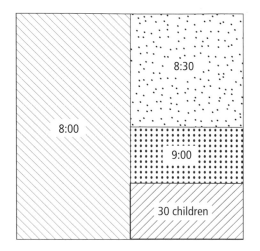

Optional adult input

Work with the More able group, asking children to explain what they have just found out and how, and what they are going to do next.

Plenary

1 **Copy the problem on Textbook page 24 on the board.**

Explain to children that they were all working on the same problem but using slightly different information.

Invite children from all groups to say how many children there were at the start of the disco (240).

Invite children from the More able group to explain how they tackled the problem. To help other children understand, occasionally get the child to elaborate by asking questions such as: *Why did you do that? How do you know that?* Encourage other children to ask questions.

2 Eventually focus on the most likely method and the one which most children should understand which is along the lines shown below. The problems that each step appears in are shown in brackets. Ask children from appropriate ability groups to explain each step. (For an alternative approach see **Useful mathematical information page 85**.)

- Step 1 (More able)
  $\frac{3}{5}$ of the children were girls, so $\frac{2}{5}$ were boys.
  There were 4 boys, so $\frac{2}{5} = 4$, so $\frac{1}{5} = 2$, so $\frac{5}{5} = 10$.
  So there were 10 children at 9:30.

- Step 2 (More able and Average)
  The 10 children represent $\frac{1}{3}$ of the children who stayed after 9:00.
  So $10 \times 3 = 30$ children stayed after 9:00.

- Step 3 (All)
  Those 30 children represent $\frac{1}{2}$ of the children who stayed after 8:30.
  So 60 children stayed after 8:30.

- Step 4 (All)
  Those 60 children represent $\frac{1}{2}$ of the children who stayed after 8:00.
  So 120 children stayed after 8:00.

- Step 5 (All)
  The 120 children represent $\frac{1}{2}$ of the children who were at the start of the disco.
  So there were 240 children at the start of the disco.

3 Discuss any difficulties with the maths that children might have experienced. Difficulties might include:

- Working out the whole amount from the fraction known, e.g. in Step 1: *If two fifths of the remaining children equals 4 children, how many remaining children were there?*

  It is important to emphasise the verbal language rather than the fraction symbols: If **two** fifths of the remaining children is 4 children, then **one** fifth of the remaining children is a half of 4 children which is 2 children. If **one** fifth of the remaining children is 2 children, then **five** fifths (all) of the remaining children is five times 2 which equals 10 children.

4 Establish that the answer can be checked by starting at the beginning of the problem with the 240 children, working through the problem, and confirming that 10 children remain at the end.

Development

Children make up similar problems for each other to solve.

Solution

There were 240 children at the start of the disco.

18 Window investigations

18 Window investigations

① Look at the square window in this 100 square.

Add the numbers in the opposite corners.

13 + 35 = ☐

15 + 33 = ☐

Double the number in the middle.

double 24 = ☐

What do you notice?

1	2	3	4	5	6	7	8	9	10
11	12	13	14	15	16	17	18	19	20
21	22	23	24	25	26	27	28	29	30
31	32	33	34	35	36	37	38	39	40
41	42	43	44	45	46	47	48	49	50
51	52	53	54	55	56	57	58	59	60
61	62	63	64	65	66	67	68	69	70
71	72	73	74	75	76	77	78	79	80
81	82	83	84	85	86	87	88	89	90
91	92	93	94	95	96	97	98	99	100

② You need a 100 square.

Draw some more 3 × 3 square windows on a 100 square.

Each time:

a add the numbers in the opposite corners;

b double the number in the middle.

③ Investigate 5 × 5 and 7 × 7 square windows.

Can you make any general statements?

④ Investigate 4 × 4 and 6 × 6 square windows.

Can you make any general statements?

25

Minimum prior experience

addition and doubling of 2-digit numbers

Resources

Pupil's Textbook page 25, PCM 8, large 100 square and multiplication square, small 100 squares and multiplication squares (from PCM 9), calculators (discretionary)

Key vocabulary

opposite, diagonally opposite, sum, total, product, double, 100 square, multiplication square, symmetrical, general statement, justify

What's the problem?

Investigations of number relationships in a 100 square and a multiplication square, involving addition and multiplication of 2-digit numbers and generalising.

Problem solving objectives

- Solve mathematical problems or puzzles, recognise and explain patterns and relationships, generalise and predict. Suggest extensions asking 'What if . . . ?'

- Make and investigate a general statement about familiar numbers or shapes by finding examples that satisfy it.

Differentiation

More able: PCM 8 Window investigations 2 (using a multiplication square)

Average: PCM 8 Window investigations 1 (similar problem, but using a 100 square)

Less able: Pupil's Textbook page 25 (similar problem to Average, but with more direction)

Introducing the problem

Display a large 100 square and a large multiplication square. Invite children to identify and discuss patterns and relationships within the squares, e.g.

- patterns formed by multiples of various numbers in both squares;

- the square numbers forming one diagonal of the multiplication square;

- the symmetry of numbers about the 'square number diagonal' in the multiplication square.

Explain to children that they will be investigating less obvious patterns in both squares. Remind them that they should record their investigations and make general statements when they think they can justify them.

Teacher focus for activity

All children: Encourage children to find the products and sums of a variety of numbers within the 'windows': opposite numbers, central numbers in 'even-sided' squares, adjacent numbers. *Which numbers have you multiplied/added so far? Have you found anything out? What other numbers could you try?*

Encourage children to investigate a particular window in different positions on the square before they make any general statements. *Can you make a general statement about numbers in all square/rectangular/cross windows? How many positions have you tried the window in? Is that enough to justify your statement? How many more do you think you need to investigate until you can be fairly sure of your statement?*

Suggest children try extremes of the shape, e.g. the complete 100 square, a 10 × 3 rectangle or a cross that spans the square.

Optional adult input

Work with the Average group. Ask children to explain any relationships they have found.

Plenary

Display a large 100 square and a large multiplication square.

1 Focus on the 100 square.
   Invite general statements about 3×3 square windows. These might include:

   - Each pair of diagonally opposite corner numbers has the same total.

   - The number in the centre of the square is half the sum of each pair of diagonally opposite numbers.

   Get children to test statements with a few 3×3 windows.

   Establish that the statements hold true also for 5×5, 7×7 and 9×9 windows. For 2×2, 4×4, 6×6 and 8×8 squares, the sums of the diagonally opposite corner numbers are equal, but there is no single central number.
   For these 'even-sided' squares, children may have noticed other relationships, e.g. the sum of the 4 central numbers equals the sum of the corner numbers.

33	34	35	36	37	38
43	44	45	46	47	48
53	54	55	56	57	58
63	64	65	66	67	68
73	74	75	76	77	78
83	84	85	86	87	88

2 Invite general statements about rectangular windows. These might include:

   - The sums of each pair of opposite corner numbers in a rectangle are always equal.

   Get children to test statements with a few rectangles.

3 Invite general statements about crosses. These might include:

   - The sums of each pair of numbers at the ends of each arm are always equal and double the number in the centre. (This applies, whatever the length of the arms, even if each arm is a different length, as long as the cross is symmetrical horizontally and vertically.)

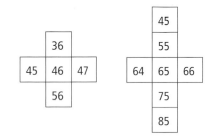

4 Deal with the multiplication square in a similar way (see **Solutions** for some general statements). Discuss similarities and differences between the 100 square and the multiplication square.

Development

Draw a 4×4 square window in a 100 square. Find the product of each pair of diagonally opposite corner numbers. Find the difference between the two products. Investigate other squares.

Solutions

(There are other possibilities for general statements.)

Textbook page 25

1 $13 + 35 = 48$; $15 + 33 = 48$; double $24 = 48$
   All three calculations give the same answer.

2 Children's own answers: sums of diagonally opposite corner numbers and doubles of centre numbers in their chosen 3×3 squares.

3 and 4 Children's own answers based on 5×5 and 7×7, then 4×4 and 6×6 squares. General statements to match those for squares in the solutions for PCM 8 Window investigations 1.

PCM 8 Window investigations 1
Squares and rectangles: The sums of diagonally opposite corner numbers are equal.
The sum of a pair of diagonally opposite corner numbers is double the centre number (in 3×3, 5×5, $7 \times 7 \ldots$ squares).
The sum of the 4 central numbers equals the sum of the corner numbers (in 4×4, 6×6, $8 \times 8 \ldots$ squares).

Crosses: The sums of each pair of opposite numbers at the ends of the arms are equal and double the number in the centre.

PCM 8 Window investigations 2
Squares and rectangles: The products of diagonally opposite corner numbers are equal.

Crosses: The sums of each pair of opposite numbers at the ends of the arms are equal and are double the number in the centre.

19 Big time

What's the problem?

Calculating the time, day, month and year it will be after a given length of time. Calculations involve converting units of time to larger units, knowledge of (or the use of) a calendar and the 4 operations, possibly with 4-digit numbers.

Problem solving objectives

- Choose and use appropriate number operations to solve problems and appropriate ways of calculating.
- Identify and use appropriate operations to solve word problems involving numbers and quantities based on 'real life', money or measures, using one or more steps.
  Explain methods and reasoning.

Differentiation

More able: PCM 10 Big time 3

Average: PCM 10 Big time 2 (similar problem, but less demanding numbers)

Less able: PCM 10 Big time 1 (similar problem, but with less demanding numbers and a hint)

Introducing the problem

Revise the number of seconds in a minute, minutes in an hour, hours in a day, days in various months and days in a year. Before children start, read through each problem with them and answer any questions they may have. Remind them that they should record

what they do, the calculations they use, and how they find the answers.

Teacher focus for activity

All children: Ask probing questions such as: *How will you tackle the problem? Talk me through it step by step. How will you work out how many minutes/hours/days/weeks that is? How could you find out how many 24s there are in that number? How could you divide by 60?*

Encourage children to devise their own methods of calculation, e.g. using a subtraction method rather than division when changing 5000 hours to days: finding out how many 24s in 5000 by taking away 24s (see **Useful mathematical information page 82**).

Less able: Make sure that children know what the time and date is at the start of a new year. Children may need to use a calendar for part **b**.

Optional adult input

Work with the Average group. Ask children to talk you through their calculations step by step. Use probing questions such as those suggested above.

Plenary

1 Focus on part **b** of Big time 1.
Invite all children to say what day it is 100 days after the start of a new year. Ask a child from the Less able group with the correct answer to explain how they arrived at the answer.

This is most likely to involve adding the number of days in January (31), February (28 or 29) and March (31), which equals 90 or 91. That leaves 10 or 9 days for April. So the answer is 12 midnight at the end of 10th April (or 9th April in a leap year).

2 Relate the previous problem to part **b** of Big time 3. Ask children from the More able group to give the answers they arrived at and to explain the methods they used. (See **Useful mathematical information pages 85–86** for 2 possible strategies.)

3 Focus on part **a** of Big time 2.
Invite all children to say at what time of what day of what year it is 2000 seconds after the start of the current year. Ask a child from the Average group with the correct answer to explain how they arrived at the answer. This will initially involve converting seconds to minutes and seconds. Possible methods of doing this should be discussed, e.g. dividing 2000 by 60 using a long division method or using a subtraction method.

The answer arrived at should be 33 minutes 20 seconds. So the time would be 12:33 am, 00:33 or, more exactly, 00:33:20 on 1st January of the current year.

Discuss the different ways of expressing the time.

4 Go over any problems children might have had with the mathematics involved. These are likely to include converting from one unit to a bigger unit which, in these problems, essentially involves division by, e.g. 60 or 24. There are several approaches, such as:

- using a standard written long division method;

- using an informal subtraction method, where multiples of the divisor are subtracted;

- using a 'building up' method where multiples of the divisor are successively added to build up the target number.

Go over each approach with the children (see **Useful mathematical information page 82**).

Development

Children calculate the number of hours, minutes or seconds in a year.

Solutions

Big time 1
a 1:40 am or 01:40 on 1st January of the current year
b 12 midnight or 00:00 at the end of 10th April (or 9th April in a leap year) of the current year

Big time 2
a 12:33 am, 00:33 or 00:33:20 on 1st January of the current year
b 9:20 am or 09:20 on 2nd January of the current year

Big time 3
a 8:00 am or 08:00 on 28th July (or 27th in a leap year) of the current year
b 12 midnight (or 00:00) at the end of 9th September in the 14th year after the start of the current year. This solution includes 3 leap years. The day will be the 8th if 4 leap years are included.

20 Patio patterns

Minimum prior experience

identifying and continuing number patterns;
identifying number relationships

Resources

Pupil's Textbook pages 26 and 27, squared paper

Key vocabulary

pattern, relationship, sequence, formula(e), rule, general statement, predict

20 Patio patterns

Jodie is making a patio.
She will make an L shape with equal-length arms from red slabs.
Then she will put a border of grey slabs around it.
Here are the 2 smallest possibilities:

arm length: 2
red slabs: 3
grey slabs: 12
total slabs: 15

arm length: 3
red slabs: 5
grey slabs: 16
total slabs: 21

1 Draw the next three patios.

2 Copy and complete this table.

arm length	2	3	4	5	6
red slabs	3	5			
grey slabs	12	16			
total slabs	15	21			

3 a Can you describe the red slabs number pattern? 3, 5 ...
  b Predict how many red slabs will be in a patio with arm length 8 slabs.

4 a Can you describe the grey slabs number pattern? 12, 16 ...
  b Predict how many grey slabs will be in a patio with arm length 9 slabs.

5 a Can you describe the total slabs number pattern? 15, 21 ...
  b Predict the total number of slabs in a patio with arm length 10 slabs.

26

What's the problem?

An algebraic investigation involving patterns and relationships which children use to make predictions and generate formulae.

Problem solving objectives

- Explain methods and reasoning, orally and in writing.
- Solve mathematical problems or puzzles, recognise and explain patterns and relationships, generalise and predict. Suggest extensions asking 'What if . . . ?'
- Make and investigate a general statement about familiar numbers or shapes by finding examples that satisfy it.
- Develop from explaining a generalised relationship in words to expressing it in a formula using letters as symbols.

Differentiation

More able: Pupil's Textbook page 27, questions 10 and 11 (an extra challenge is also provided)

Average: Pupil's Textbook page 27, questions 6 to 9 (same problem, but identifying a simpler relationship). Children could move on to question 11.

Less able: Pupil's Textbook page 26, questions 1 to 5 (same problem, but making specific predictions). Children could move on to question 8.

Introducing the problem

Does anyone have a patio in their garden? Are the slabs in a pattern? Go over the problem introduction on Textbook page 26. Establish that 'arm length' means the number of slabs in each arm of a red ⌊ shape.

Explain that children will use patios to create number patterns. They will investigate relationships and use them to make predictions about larger patios.

Remind children that they should record their working clearly.

Teacher focus for activity

All children: When describing patterns, encourage children to do more than merely look at the difference between consecutive numbers. *What is special about the numbers in this sequence? Why do you think all the numbers are odd? . . . multiples of 4? . . .*

More able: Children may find it helpful to look at the patio pictures to identify the relationship between arm length and total slabs. *What stays the same in each picture?* (e.g. Each patio is a square with a square piece missing from the top right corner.) *What increases each time?* (side lengths of the square and the 'missing' piece) *By how much?* (by 1) *Is there a relationship each time between the arm length and the square?* (side length of square is arm length plus 2) . . . *the arm length and the 'missing' piece?* (side length of missing piece is arm length minus 1)

(For more about these relationships see **Useful mathematical information pages 86–87**.)

Optional adult input

Work with the More able group. Ask children to explain what they have found out and what they are going to investigate next.

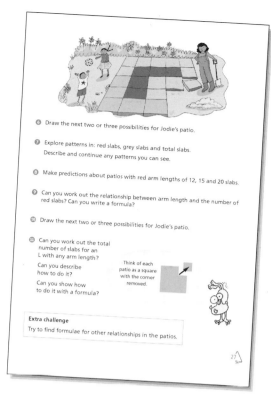

6 Draw the next two or three possibilities for Jodie's patio.

7 Explore patterns in: red slabs, grey slabs and total slabs. Describe and continue any patterns you can see.

8 Make predictions about patios with red arm lengths of 12, 15 and 20 slabs.

9 Can you work out the relationship between arm length and the number of red slabs? Can you write a formula?

10 Draw the next two or three possibilities for Jodie's patio.

11 Can you work out the total number of slabs for an L with any arm length?

Can you describe how to do it?

Can you show how to do it with a formula?

Think of each patio as a square with the corner removed.

Extra challenge
Try to find formulae for other relationships in the patios.

Plenary

1 **Draw the first few patios and the incomplete table from Textbook page 26.**

Ask children to help you complete the table. Discuss patterns in each row and the types of number they contain.

arm length	2	3	4	5	6
red slabs	3	5	7	9	11
grey slabs	12	16	20	24	28
total slabs	15	21	27	33	39

add 2; the sequence of odd numbers starting from 3

add 4; the sequence of multiples of 4 starting from 12

add 6; all multiples of 3

2 *What is the relationship between arm length and the number of red slabs?* (e.g. The number of red slabs is twice the arm length minus 1.)
Can you express this relationship as a formula? (e.g. $R = 2L - 1$, where R is the number of red slabs and L is the arm length)

Use patio pictures to discuss the reasons for this relationship. (Each red ⌊ shape has 2 arms, so the number of slabs would be twice the arm length ($2L$), except there is one slab common to both arms, so we must subtract a slab.)

3 Ask if any children managed to find a way of calculating the total number of slabs for any arm length. Here are 2 possibilities:

- Add 2 to the arm length and square the answer. Subtract 1 from the arm length and square the answer. Subtract the second answer from the first answer:
  $$T = (L + 2)^2 - (L - 1)^2$$

- Multiply the arm length by 6 and add 3:
  $$T = 6L + 3$$

With children, test the formulae on patios with different arm lengths.

Can children use patio pictures to explain the relationships? (See **Useful mathematical information pages 86–87**.)

Development

Children investigate 'T' shaped patios.

Solutions

The next 3 patios:

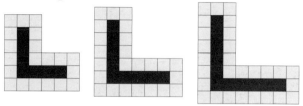

1 See patio diagrams.
2 See table in **Plenary**.
3 a As question **7** (red) b 15
4 a As question **7** (grey) b 40
5 a As question **7** (total) b 63

6 See patio diagrams.
7 Red: the sequence of odd numbers starting from 3; 'add 2'
Grey: the sequence of multiples of 4 starting from 12; 'add 4'
Total: all multiples of 3; 'add 6'

8

arm length	12	15	20
red	23	29	39
grey	52	64	84
total	75	93	123

9 The number of red slabs is twice the arm length minus 1: $R = 2L - 1$

10 See patio diagrams.
11 Add 2 to the arm length and square the answer. Subtract 1 from the arm length and square the answer. Subtract the second answer from the first answer:
$$T = (L + 2)^2 - (L - 1)^2$$
or multiply the arm length by 6 and add 3:
$$T = 6L + 3$$
Extra challenge: children's own answers about other relationships in the patios

21 Broken calculators

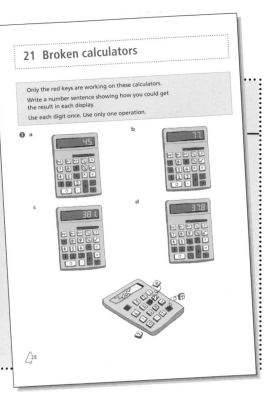

21 Broken calculators

Only the red keys are working on these calculators.

Write a number sentence showing how you could get the result in each display.

Use each digit once. Use only one operation.

a   b

c   d

28

Minimum prior experience

calculator use; the four operations with 2- or 3-digit numbers

Resources

Pupil's Textbook pages 28 and 29

Key vocabulary

calculation, operation, reasonable, estimate, approximate, trial and improvement

What's the problem?

Problems in the context of calculators with 'broken' keys involving approximation, decimals, reasoning about numbers and an understanding of the 4 operations and their relationships.

Problem solving objectives

- Choose and use appropriate number operations to solve problems and appropriate ways of calculating.

- Solve mathematical problems or puzzles, recognise and explain patterns and relationships, generalise and predict. Suggest extensions asking 'What if . . . ?'

Differentiation

More able: Pupil's Textbook page 29, problem 3

Average: Pupil's Textbook page 29, problem 2 (same problem, but with less demanding numbers)

Less able: Pupil's Textbook page 28, problem 1 (same problem, but with even less demanding numbers)

Introducing the problem

Read through the instructions at the top of Textbook page 28, ensuring that children understand them. Explain that you expect them to think carefully about the numbers involved and use what they know about numbers and number operations to arrive at the solutions.

Teacher focus for activity

All children: Encourage children to reason about numbers without inadvertently giving them clues. Ask questions such as:

Which operation do you think it definitely could not be? Why?

Which operation do you think it could be? Why?

Which numbers would definitely not give the answer? Why?

Which numbers do you think might give this result? Why?

What calculations have you tried so far? Why did you try that calculation first?

Encourage children to keep a record of the calculations they have tried, to avoid repetition.

Optional adult input

Work with the More able group. Ask children to talk you through what they have done so far. Ask them to explain why they thought particular calculations might produce the required answer.

Plenary

Write the number in the calculator display and the red key digits and signs for the first part of each problem on the board.

1 Deal with 1a first. (answer: 45; red keys: $\boxed{1}$ $\boxed{2}$ $\boxed{6}$ $\boxed{9}$ $\boxed{+}$ $\boxed{-}$ $\boxed{=}$)

Ask children whether the calculation could be subtraction and discuss the reasons why it could or could not be. (e.g. Although subtracting a

3 Deal with 3a in a similar way. (answer: 94.15; red keys: 1 3 4 5 7 × + − · =)

Considering addition or subtraction, one of the numbers must have 2 decimal places. This being the case, quick approximations will indicate that 94.15 cannot possibly be obtained by either operation.

Consider multiplication. To produce an answer ending in 5 means that one of the numbers must end with 5 and the other with an odd digit or vice versa. (The product of an even number and 5 always ends with zero.) Estimation can then be used to find likely solutions. Some likely solutions are: 13.45 × 7; 13.47 × 5; 17.43 × 5. Actual calculation will confirm that the solution is 13.45 × 7

Development

Children make up broken calculator problems for each other.

Solutions

1 a 19 + 26 (corresponding digits in each number are interchangeable)
   b 94 − 17
   c 127 × 3
   d 12.6 × 3

2 a 6.57 × 8
   b 13.6 × 5 (Note: 63 + 5 and 65 + 3 do not use **each** digit)
   c 2.45 + 6.37 (corresponding digits in each number are interchangeable)
   d 14.7 ÷ 3

3 a 13.45 × 7
   b 56.1 ÷ 3
   c 1.35 + 9.48 (corresponding digits in each number are interchangeable)
   d 48.52 − 39.06

---

number with 1 unit from a number with 6 units – or vice versa – would result in 5 units, it is not possible to produce 4 tens using the remaining keys 1 and 2.)

Establish, therefore, that the operation must be addition. Discuss any clues there are as to which numbers are added, e.g. the units digits in the two numbers must be 9 and 6 because they are the only ones that would produce the required 5 units in the answer.

Establish that the numbers must be 16 and 29, or 26 and 19. So the calculation is either 16 + 29 or 26 + 19.

2 Deal with 2a in a similar way. (answer: 52.56; red keys: 5 6 7 8 × + − · =)

By considering possibilities for the final digit 6 and considering the number of digits in the answer, establish that the operation cannot be addition or subtraction, so it must be multiplication.

What clues could we use to help us decide on which 2 numbers are multiplied? Discuss children's responses and their reasoning. (e.g. The only two digits whose product ends in 6 are 7 and 8, so one number must end in 7, and the other in 8.) If we investigate multiplication by an integer, the possibilities are 5.68 × 7, 6.58 × 7, 5.67 × 8 or 6.57 × 8

Using a combination of approximation and calculation we arrive at 6.57 × 8

22 Bargain trainers

Minimum prior experience

simple fractions and percentages of money

Resources

Pupil's Textbook page 30, PCM 11

Key vocabulary

percentage discount, reduction, equivalent fraction, per cent (%), sale price

22 Bargain trainers

The Super Sports shop is holding a sale of Zoom trainers for 1 week.

Monday: **ZOOM** trainers REDUCED by 20%

Tuesday: **25% DISCOUNT** on Yesterday's PRICE

Wednesday: **50% DISCOUNT ON TUESDAY'S** PRICE

Thursday: **REDUCTION** of 10% ON Wednesday's PRICE

Friday: A FURTHER £2.99 **ZOOM** Trainers Now only £22.5

What was the original price of the trainers?

Start from Friday and work backwards. What was the price of trainers on Thursday? What percentage of Wednesday's price is Thursday's price?

30

What's the problem?

Calculating the original price of an item given a series of percentage discounts and the final price (or the final price given the original price, in the case of the Less able activity).

Problem solving objectives:

- Choose and use appropriate number operations to solve problems, and appropriate ways of calculating.

- Identify and use appropriate operations to solve word problems involving numbers and quantities based on 'real life' or money using one or more steps. Explain methods and reasoning.

Differentiation

More able: PCM 11 Bargain trainers 2

Average: Pupil's Textbook page 30 (same problem, but with fewer stages and with clues)

Less able: PCM 11 Bargain trainers 1 (similar problem, but using the given original price to find the final price)

Introducing the problem

Revise the meaning of per cent (one in every 100). Revise equivalence between common percentages and fractions, e.g. $50\% = \frac{1}{2}$; $25\% = \frac{1}{4}$; $75\% = \frac{3}{4}$; $10\% = \frac{1}{10}$; $20\% = \frac{2}{10}$ or $\frac{1}{5}$. Explain to children that the problem this lesson involves using percentages in the context of a sale. Tell them that they should record all their working. Allow children a few minutes to read through their problem and ask questions before they start.

Teacher focus for activity

More able: Discuss with children how they will tackle the problem. For children finding it difficult to start, ask questions that direct them towards the end of the problem, e.g. *What is the final price of the trainers? How could we work out Friday's price? What do we know that would help us? What percentage of Friday's price is £22.50?* (90% **not** 10%)

Average: If necessary, go through the clues at the bottom of the page. Look out for children who think that Thursday's price is 10% of Wednesday's price rather than a **reduction** of 10% on Wednesday's price (so 90% of Wednesday's price).

Less able: Make sure that children understand the fractional equivalence of the various percentages and can calculate simple fractions of money. Make sure that they understand that once the discount has been calculated it needs to be subtracted from the original price to obtain the new sale price.

Optional adult input

Work with the Less able group. Make sure that the answer for each day of the sale is correct before they move on to the next day.

Plenary

1 Briefly focus on PCM 11 Bargain trainers 1. Explain that all the problems are based on similar data. Sale prices for each day are the same in each problem so they can all check their answers as Bargain trainers 1 is worked through.

Start with the original price for the trainers of £100 and ask children to calculate the percentage discount and price of trainers for each day of the sale, explaining how they did it. Establish daily sale prices as follows:

Monday: £80; Tuesday: £60; Wednesday: £30; Thursday: £27; Friday: £25

For example, to calculate Monday's price:

The full price is reduced by 20%
1% of £100 is £1, so 20% is £1 × 20 = £20
So the sale price is £100 − £20 = £80

or

The full price is reduced by 20%
20% is equivalent to $\frac{1}{5}$
$\frac{1}{5}$ of £100 is £100 ÷ 5 = £20
So the sale price is £100 − £20 = £80

(See **Useful mathematical information page 87** for more information about finding percentages.)

2 Focus on PCM 11 Bargain trainers 2 and Textbook page 30.
Establish that one way to solve both problems was to start with the final sale price and work backwards day by day up to the original price. Explain that Bargain trainers 2 included a further reduction on Saturday of 10% giving a sale price of £22.50

Work through the problem step by step, asking children to explain how to calculate each day's sale price and discussing their responses. Responses are likely to be along the following lines:

● Friday's price
Saturday's price of £22.50 is a result of a 10% discount on Friday's price.
So £22.50 must represent 90% of Friday's price.
If 90% (or $\frac{9}{10}$) of Friday's price is £22.50, then 10% (or $\frac{1}{10}$) is £22.50 ÷ 9 = £2.50
So 100% (or $\frac{10}{10}$) of Friday's price is £2.50 × 10 = £25. Friday's price is £25.

Discuss the different ways in which children may have divided £22.50 by 9. These could include: doing a standard written division with the amount as it is; converting the £22.50 to pence (2250p) before dividing; noticing that, conveniently, there are nine lots of £2.50 in £22.50.

● Thursday's price
Friday's price of £25 is a reduction of £2 on Thursday's price. So Thursday's price must be £25 + £2 = £27

● Wednesday's price
Thursday's price of £27 is a result of a 10% discount on Wednesday's price.
So £27 represents 90% of Wednesday's price.
If 90% (or $\frac{9}{10}$) of Wednesday's price is £27 then 10% (or $\frac{1}{10}$) is £27 ÷ 9 = £3
So 100% (or $\frac{10}{10}$) of Wednesday's price is £3 × 10 = £30. Wednesday's price is £30.

● Tuesday's and Monday's prices and the original price
These can be calculated using similar methods to those used for other days of the week.

● Saving on the original price
Once the original price is known, then the amount saved by buying in the sale on Saturday can be calculated (£100 − £22.50 = £77.50).

Development

What is the total percentage discount off the original price of trainers bought on Tuesday? . . . Wednesday? . . . Thursday? . . . Friday? . . . Saturday?

Solutions

PCM 11 Bargain trainers 1
£25

PCM 11 Bargain trainers 2
£77.50

Textbook page 30
£100

23 Fields and rectangles

23 Fields and rectangles

① The perimeter of this rectangle is 30 cm.

length = 11 cm   width = 4 cm   area = 44 cm²

a How many different rectangles can you draw with a perimeter of 30 cm?
Write underneath each one the length, the width and the area.

b What is the biggest area possible for a rectangle with a perimeter of 30 cm?

② a A farmer has 30 metres of fence to enclose some land.
What is the largest rectangular area she can enclose?

b What if she is able to use a wall as 1 side of the enclosure?
What is the maximum area she can enclose now?

31

Minimum prior experience

area of rectangles by counting squares; perimeters

Resources

Pupil's Textbook page 31, large grid of squares (optional), centimetre squared paper, calculators (discretionary)

Key vocabulary

perimeter, area, rectangle, square, rectangular, square centimetre, pattern

What's the problem?

Investigating areas of rectangles with the same perimeter and finding the rectangle with the largest area. The investigation involves reasoning about numbers and identifying patterns, and may include fractional areas and calculating with fractions.

Problem solving objectives

- Explain methods and reasoning, orally and in writing.
- Solve mathematical problems or puzzles, recognise and explain patterns and relationships, generalise and predict. Suggest extensions asking 'What if . . . ?'

Differentiation

More able: Pupil's Textbook page 31, problem 2

Average: Pupil's Textbook page 31, problem 2 (same problem, differentiation by outcome)

Less able: Pupil's Textbook page 31, problem 1 (similar problem, but with more guidance)

Introducing the problem

Revise the meanings of 'perimeter' (the distance all the way around a shape) and 'area' (the amount of surface contained within a shape). Children should then start on the problems straight away.

Teacher focus on activity

More able and Average: Organising and ordering the data is a key strategy for solving this problem. However, do not suggest this to children directly. Instead, ask probing questions such as: *Can you give me the length and width of a rectangle with a perimeter of 30 metres? How did you work that out? Can you give me another example? What are the other possibilities? How do you know this is the rectangle with the largest area? What is the rectangle with the smallest area? Can you think of one that might have a smaller area?*

Children who decide to include areas of rectangles with fractional dimensions, e.g. 6.5 m × 8.5 m, may find it helpful to draw the rectangles on squared paper.

Less able: Ask questions such as: *How will you work out the length and width of a rectangle with a perimeter of 30 cm? How can you make sure that you have as many different rectangles as possible?*

Optional adult input

Work with the Less able group. Help children to understand that length plus width equals half the perimeter. Help them to find all possible rectangles with whole number side lengths.

Plenary

It would be useful to have a display grid of squares on which rectangles can be drawn.

1 Focus on the first part of problem 2. Explain that everyone has been investigating rectangles with a perimeter of 30, but some have been thinking about 30 centimetres and others about 30 metres.

Discuss the various approaches. Discuss each approach in terms of efficiency and making the identification of patterns easier. One likely systematic approach is as follows (there may be others):

Establish first that the length plus breadth of each rectangle must equal half the perimeter, i.e. 15 metres.

Systematically list the whole-number dimensions of all rectangles where the sum of the length and width is 15 metres, together with their area:
1 m × 14 m = 14 m²; 2 m × 13 m = 26 m²;
3 m × 12 m = 36 m²; 4 m × 11 m = 44 m²;
5 m × 10 m = 50 m²; 6 m × 9 m = 54 m²;
7 m × 8 m = 56 m²; 8 m × 7 m = 56 m²...

Children should notice that:

- the areas increase as the difference between the length and width decreases;
- rectangles start repeating after 7 m × 8 m;
- the difference between consecutive areas decreases by 2 m² each time.

It may appear that the maximum area is 56 m².

2 If nobody else suggests it, ask: *Could there be a bigger area if we included dimensions with fractions of a metre? What could we try? Why?*
It could be reasoned that as the areas increased up to 7 m × 8 m and decreased after 8 m × 7 m, if there is a bigger area it would be between these two rectangles.

Establish that a $7\frac{1}{2}$ m × $7\frac{1}{2}$ m (or 7.5 m × 7.5 m) square fits 'half way' between these two rectangles. (Some children may need reminding that a square is just a special kind of rectangle.)

Ask children for suggestions as to how the area could be calculated.
Other than using a calculator, this area could be found in one of two ways:

- by drawing a $7\frac{1}{2} \times 7\frac{1}{2}$ rectangle on a grid of squares and counting squares and fractions of a square to find the area;

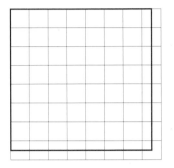

- by reasoning about fractions:
$7\frac{1}{2}$ sevens = 7 sevens + $\frac{1}{2}$ a seven = $49 + 3\frac{1}{2} = 52\frac{1}{2}$
$7\frac{1}{2}$ halves = 7 halves + $\frac{1}{2}$ a half = $3\frac{1}{2}$ and $\frac{1}{4} = 3\frac{3}{4}$
So $7\frac{1}{2}$ seven and a halves = $52\frac{1}{2} + 3\frac{3}{4} = 56\frac{1}{4}$

Establish that the maximum rectangular area that the farmer could enclose with 30 metres of fencing is 56.25 m² or $56\frac{1}{4}$ m².

Development

Children investigate whether the maximum area for a rectangle of given perimeter is always a square.

Solutions

1 a 7 different rectangles (if only whole number side lengths are used)
Dimensions and areas: 1 cm × 14 cm (14 cm²);
2 cm × 13 cm (26 cm²); 3 cm × 12 cm (36 cm²);
4 cm × 11 cm (44 cm²); 5 cm × 10 cm (50 cm²);
6 cm × 9 cm (54 cm²); 7 cm × 8 cm (56 cm²)
b 56 cm² (for sides with a whole number of centimetres)

2 a 56.25 m²   **b** 100 m²

24 Handshakes

Minimum prior experience

identifying and continuing number patterns;
identifying number relationships

Resources

Pupil's Textbook pages 32 and 33

Key vocabulary

pattern, relationship, sequence, formula, rule, predict, triangular number, general statement

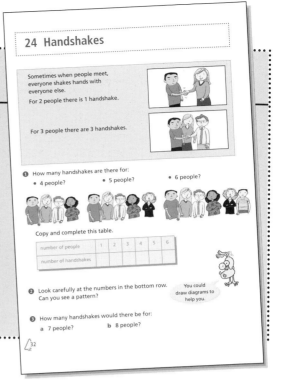

24 Handshakes

Sometimes when people meet, everyone shakes hands with everyone else.
For 2 people there is 1 handshake.

For 3 people there are 3 handshakes.

❶ How many handshakes are there for:
• 4 people?   • 5 people?   • 6 people?

Copy and complete this table.

number of people	1	2	3	4	5	6
number of handshakes						

❷ Look carefully at the numbers in the bottom row. Can you see a pattern?

You could draw diagrams to help you.

❸ How many handshakes would there be for:
a 7 people?   b 8 people?

32

What's the problem?

An algebraic investigation using patterns of numbers to make predictions and perhaps to derive a formula.

Problem solving objectives

- Explain methods and reasoning, orally and in writing.
- Solve mathematical problems or puzzles, recognise and explain patterns and relationships, generalise and predict. Suggest extensions asking 'What if . . . ?'
- Make and investigate a general statement about familiar numbers or shapes by finding examples that satisfy it.
- Develop from explaining a generalised relationship in words to expressing it in a formula using letters as symbols.

Differentiation

More able: Pupil's Textbook page 33, question 7

Average: Pupil's Textbook page 33, questions 4 to 6 (same problem, but with more guidance and less demanding predictions)

Less able: Pupil's Textbook page 32, questions 1 to 3 (same problem as Average, but with less demanding predictions). Where appropriate, children could move on to question 6.

Introducing the problem

To introduce the problem, explain that in some cultures, when a group of people meet, it is considered polite for everyone to shake hands with everyone else.

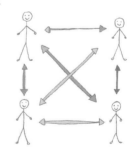

Using children to illustrate, establish that if there are just 2 people then there will be 1 handshake and if there are 3 people there will be 3 handshakes. Invite children to predict how many handshakes there will be for 4 people. At this stage do not confirm which answer is correct.

Explain that in this lesson, children will be investigating the number of handshakes for various numbers of people.

Teacher focus for activity

All children: Children may find it helpful to draw diagrams to represent the handshakes. Ask questions about consecutive numbers of handshakes: *Can you see a pattern? Can you describe it to me? Have you seen this pattern of numbers before?*

More able: Help children to arrive at a generalisation by asking questions such as: *Do people shake hands with themselves? How many people does each person shake hands with? So how many handshakes is that for everybody? Is that the total number of handshakes then?*

Optional adult input

Work with the Less able group. Help children to draw diagrams to represent the numbers of handshakes for

Investigate the number of handshakes for different numbers of people. Enter your results in a table like this:

number of people	1	2	3	4	5	6	7	8
number of handshakes								

5 Can you see a pattern in the numbers of handshakes? Try to describe it.

6 Use the pattern to predict the number of handshakes for:

a 10 people b 15 people c 20 people

7 Investigate the number of handshakes for different numbers of people. Can you find any relationship between the number of people and the number of handshakes?

Can you find a method of working out how many handshakes for:

• 50 people? • any number of people?

Can you work out a formula that will give the number of handshakes for any number of people?

33

4, 5 and 6 people. You may want to ask the appropriate number of children to shake hands with each other in order to help with the drawings or to check the results.

Plenary

1 Draw the incomplete table on the board.

number of people	1	2	3	4	5	6
number of handshakes						

Invite children to help you complete the table. As they do so, ask them to describe any patterns they can see in the bottom row.

They may notice that the difference between consecutive numbers of handshakes increases by one each time. Some children may also notice that the numbers in the bottom row are triangular numbers (see **Useful mathematical information pages 82–83**).

2 When the table is complete, invite children to use the pattern to predict the number of handshakes for 7, 8, 9, 10 . . . people.
Could we work out the number of handshakes for, say, 100 people or 236 people in this way? Establish that you could but that it would be very time consuming to extend the sequence that far.

3 Ask if any children can make a general statement about the relationship between the number of people and the number of handshakes (e.g. The number of handshakes is the number of people, multiplied by one less than the number of people, divided by 2).

Ask children to explain how they arrived at the statement. (e.g. Everyone shakes hands with everyone but themselves, but each handshake is shared by 2 people.)

Ask children to use known examples to confirm this general statement.

Invite children to express the statement as a formula, e.g. $H = (P \times (P - 1)) \div 2$, where H is the number of handshakes and P is the number of people.

Ask children to use the formula to predict the number of handshakes for different numbers of people, such as 25, 50, 100.

(See **Useful mathematical information page 87** for more information on deriving the general statement and formula.)

Development

Children calculate the number of handshakes for a sports team, their class, the whole school or their town.

Solutions

1

number of people	1	2	3	4	5	6
number of handshakes	0	1	3	6	10	15

2 The difference between consecutive numbers of handshakes increases by 1 each time; they are the triangular numbers.

3 a 21 handshakes **b** 28 handshakes

4

number of people	1	2	3	4	5	6	7	8
number of handshakes	0	1	3	6	10	15	21	28

5 Same answer as question **2**.

6 10 people: 45 handshakes;
15 people: 105 handshakes;
20 people: 190 handshakes.

7 The number of handshakes for any number of people could be worked out as follows:
The number of people, multiplied by one less than the number of people, divided by 2 (so for 50 people the number of handshakes is $(50 \times 49) \div 2 = 1225$).
This gives the formula:
$H = (P \times (P - 1)) \div 2$, where H is the number of handshakes and P is the number of people.

25 Average scores

Minimum prior experience

finding the mean, mode, median and range of a set of data

Resources

Pupil's Textbook pages 34 and 35, counters or small cubes

Key vocabulary

average, mean, mode, median, range, data, order, middle value, trial and improvement

For each problem, find as many possibilities as you can.

1 **a** Chumley school have played 5 netball matches.

Their median score is 4.
Their lowest score is 2.
Their highest score is 5.

What could the five scores be?

b Chortley school have played 4 netball matches.

Their mode score is 4.
Their range of scores is 5.

What could the four scores be?

c Cherley school have played 3 football matches.

Their mean score is 5.
Their median score is 5.

What could the three scores be?

34

What's the problem?

Reasoning the possible scores from information about the mean, mode, median and range of a set of scores.

Problem solving objectives

- Choose and use appropriate number operations to solve problems and appropriate ways of calculating.
- Solve mathematical problems or puzzles, recognise and explain patterns and relationships, generalise and predict. Suggest extensions asking 'What if . . . ?'
- Identify and use appropriate operations to solve word problems involving numbers and quantities based on 'real life', using one or more steps. Explain methods and reasoning.

Differentiation

More able: Pupil's Textbook page 35, problem 2

Average: Pupil's Textbook page 35, problem 2 (same problem, but with discretionary clues)

Less able: Pupil's Textbook page 34, problem 1 (similar problem, but with less demanding numbers)

Introducing the problem

Write these 'test' marks on the board: 5, 6, 2, 6, 1

Use the marks to revise the meanings of mode, mean, median and range. Explain that in this lesson, children will be given information about the mode, median, mean and range of a set of data and will be asked to work out what the data could have been.

Teacher focus for activity

More able and Average: Only to those children who are struggling, suggest that they start with a baseline of 5 scores of 8 and then make adjustments to the scores to meet the mean, mode, median and range criteria.

(Discretionary clues for Average) If necessary use questions as hints, e.g. *What is the total of their scores?* (40) *Must that stay the same? Why? What else must stay the same?* (the median and mode and range) *If their lowest score was 1, what must their highest score be?* (10) *What must their middle score be?*

Children may find it helpful to represent scores with piles of counters or cubes.

Less able: For each problem, help children establish a baseline of known scores from which to work, e.g. with part **a**, the baseline is 2 ? 4 ? 5. Then it is a matter of working out what the unknowns could be.

Encourage children to be systematic.

Optional adult input

Work with the More able and Average groups. Get children to check the mean, mode, median and range of each set of data they arrive at.

70

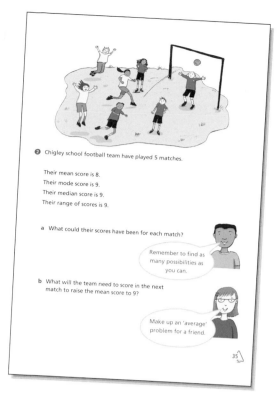

❷ Chigley school football team have played 5 matches.

Their mean score is 8.
Their mode score is 9.
Their median score is 9.
Their range of scores is 9.

a What could their scores have been for each match?

Remember to find as many possibilities as you can.

b What will the team need to score in the next match to raise the mean score to 9?

Make up an 'average' problem for a friend.

35

Plenary

1 Focus on problem 2. The Less able group will be able to contribute, particularly when dealing with the mode, median and range of a set of data.

Invite children to explain how they tackled the problem.

One likely approach is to start with a baseline of five ordered scores. These can be fairly random, or could be five scores of 8 (the mean score). Adjustments can be made from there to meet the criteria for mode, median and range.

During the course of discussion, establish that because the mean score is 8 and there are five matches, the total score is 40 (5 × 8). So whatever the individual scores are, the total score must remain at 40 to maintain a mean score of 8. Subtracting from one score must be balanced by distributing the same amount between the other scores.

Starting with a baseline of 8, 8, 8, 8, 8, the procedure might be as follows:

- Fix the middle (median) score at 9 and make an adjustment elsewhere to maintain the total of 40: 7, 8, 9, 8, 8.

- We know that the mode score is 9 so there must be at least two 9s. So change an 8 to a 9 and adjust the 7 to keep the total 40: 6, 8, 9, 9, 8.

- Adjust the first and last scores so that they have a difference of 9 (the range), e.g. 0, 8, 9, 9, 9.

The range is right. The median and mode are right, but the total is now only 35. So suitable adjustments have to be made to return the total to 40. And so on.

Once one solution has been found then the minimum and maximum scores can be increased or decreased in steps of 1, and the other solutions (3 in all) found.

2 Point out to children that this approach to problem solving is known as 'trial and improvement'.

3 Invite children to give the answer to part b of problem 2 and explain their reasoning. The reasoning is likely to be along the following lines:

- After the next match there will be six scores.

- For a mean score of 9, the total of the scores needs to be 6 × 9 = 54

- The current total score is 40.

- So the team will need to score 54 − 40 = 14 goals to raise the mean score to 9.

Development

If the range of scores for the first five matches is 12, what are the possible scores now?

Solutions

1 a 2, 2, 4, 4, 5;   2, 2, 4, 5, 5;   2, 3, 4, 4, 5;
   2, 3, 4, 5, 5;   2, 4, 4, 4, 5;   2, 4, 4, 5, 5
  b 0, 4, 4, 5;   1, 4, 4, 6;   2, 4, 4, 7;
   3, 4, 4, 8;   4, 4, 4, 9
  c 0, 5, 10;   1, 5, 9;   2, 5, 8;
   3, 5, 7;   4, 5, 6;   5, 5, 5

2 a 2, 9, 9, 9, 11;   3, 7, 9, 9, 12;   4, 5, 9, 9, 13
  b 14 goals

26 Cuboid frames

Minimum prior experience

perimeters of rectangles; properties of cuboids

Resources

Pupil's Textbook pages 36 and 37, calculators (discretionary)

Key vocabulary

perimeter, cuboid, cube, edge, face, pattern, formula, rule, systematic

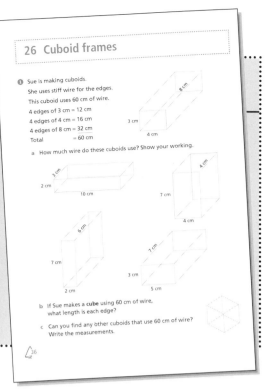

26 Cuboid frames

Sue is making cuboids.
She uses stiff wire for the edges.
This cuboid uses 60 cm of wire.
4 edges of 3 cm = 12 cm
4 edges of 4 cm = 16 cm
4 edges of 8 cm = 32 cm
Total   = 60 cm

a   How much wire do these cuboids use? Show your working.

b   If Sue makes a **cube** using 60 cm of wire, what length is each edge?

c   Can you find any other cuboids that use 60 cm of wire? Write the measurements.

36

What's the problem?

An investigation of cuboids involving an understanding of perimeter, reasoning about the properties of cuboids, identifying patterns and making predictions.

Problem solving objectives

● Explain methods and reasoning, orally and in writing.

● Solve mathematical problems or puzzles, recognise and explain patterns and relationships, generalise and predict. Suggest extensions asking 'What if . . . ?

Differentiation

More able: Pupil's Textbook page 37, problem 2

Average: Pupil's Textbook page 37, problem 2 (same problem, differentiation by outcome)

Less able: Pupil's Textbook page 36, problem 1 (same problem, but with closed questions as examples before the more open investigation)

Introducing the problem

Revise the properties of cuboids (e.g. numbers of faces, edges and vertices; that opposite faces are identical). Explain that the problems in this lesson involve skeletal cuboids (cuboid frames). Advise children to try to work systematically and to record all their working. Children then start on the problems.

Teacher focus for activity

All children: Discuss ways in which total lengths of wire can be calculated, e.g. by multiplying each dimension by 4 and adding, or by adding each dimension and multiplying by 4.

More able and Average: Discuss with children systematic ways of investigating. You could suggest fixing one dimension at 1 cm and investigating all the possible variations for the other 2 dimensions, then doing the same with a fixed dimension of 2 cm . . . Discuss any patterns that children see emerging in their recordings.

Look out for duplications in the cuboids children record. Discuss why they are duplications, e.g. a cuboid with a length, width and height of 4 cm, 8 cm and 3 cm respectively is essentially the same as a cuboid with a length, width and height of 3 cm, 4 cm and 8 cm respectively.

Optional adult input

Work with the Less able group. Make sure children understand the example at the beginning of their problem. Encourage them to record the total lengths of the edges of the cuboids as in the example.

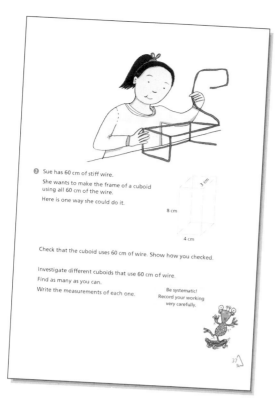

Plenary

1 Ask children from all groups to give you the length, breadth and height of cuboids that use 60 centimetres of wire. Sketch one of the cuboids and write in the dimensions.

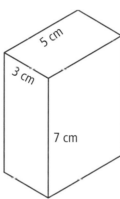

Ask children to suggest ways of checking the total length of wire used for each cuboid.

One method is to multiply each dimension by 4 and add the products. For a cuboid whose dimensions are 3 cm, 5 cm and 7 cm, the total length of edges is:

$(3 \text{ cm} \times 4) + (5 \text{ cm} \times 4) + (7 \text{ cm} \times 4) =$
$12 \text{ cm} + 20 \text{ cm} + 28 \text{ cm} = 60 \text{ cm}$

Alternatively, the dimensions could be added first and then multiplied by 4. For the example above, the total length of the edges is given by:

$(3 \text{ cm} + 5 \text{ cm} + 7 \text{ cm}) \times 4 = 15 \text{ cm} \times 4 = 60 \text{ cm}$

Ask children to use one of the methods to check the total length of edges of each cuboid.

Ask if anyone managed to find the 19 possible cuboids.

2 Ask children to explain any systematic approaches they used for the investigation.
Here is one approach (there are others):

- Because there are 4 length edges, 4 width edges and 4 height edges, adding each dimension and multiplying the total by 4 will give the total length of all the edges.

- If the total length of the edges is to be 60 cm, then the sum of the dimensions must always be 15 cm, because 15 cm × 4 = 60 cm

- If we fix one of the dimensions at 1 cm then the sum of the other two must be 14 cm. So the possible dimensions are:
  1 cm, 1 cm, 13 cm; 1 cm, 2 cm, 12 cm;
  1 cm, 3 cm, 11 cm; 1 cm, 4 cm, 10 cm;
  1 cm, 5 cm, 9 cm; 1 cm, 6 cm, 8 cm;
  1 cm, 7 cm, 7 cm

(The dimensions of the next cuboid would be 1 cm, 8 cm, 6 cm. Establish that this is essentially the same as the previous cuboid with dimensions 1 cm, 6 cm, 8 cm. Show that continuing this pattern just produces repeat cuboids.)

- If we now fix one of the dimensions at 2 cm, the sum of the other two dimensions must be 13 cm. So, repeating the process produces:
  2 cm, 2 cm, 11 cm; 2 cm, 3 cm, 10 cm;
  2 cm, 4 cm, 9 cm . . .

- Then list cuboids with a fixed edges of 3 cm, 4 cm and 5 cm.

- Children should notice that fixing an edge at 6 cm just produces duplications.

  List all the solutions. Ask children from the Less able group which of the cuboids is a cube. (5 cm, 5 cm, 5 cm)

Development

Children identify the cuboid that will contain the most/fewest centimetre cubes.

Solutions

1 a Each cuboid uses 60 cm of wire.
  b 5 cm
  c Any sets of dimensions from Problem **2** (other than 2, 3, 10; 2, 6, 7; 3, 5, 7; 4, 4, 7; 5, 5, 5 which have already been used in parts **a** and **b**).

2 1, 1, 13; 1, 2, 12; 1, 3, 11; 1, 4, 10; 1, 5, 9; 1, 6, 8; 1, 7, 7; 2, 2, 11; 2, 3, 10; 2, 4, 9; 2, 5, 8; 2, 6, 7; 3, 3, 9; 3, 4, 8 (example in Textbook); 3, 5, 7; 3, 6, 6; 4, 4, 7; 4, 5, 6; 5, 5, 5

27 Grid squares

Minimum prior experience

identifying number patterns

Resources

Pupil's Textbook page 38, PCM 12, chessboard (or an 8×8 chequered grid), square grids of various sizes from 2×2 to 8×8, calculators

Key vocabulary

pattern, sequence, multiple, rule, predict, square number

What's the problem?

An investigation of square grids involving the identification of patterns and square numbers, and generalising.

Problem solving objectives

- Explain methods and reasoning, orally and in writing.
- Solve mathematical problems or puzzles, recognise and explain patterns and relationships, generalise and predict. Suggest extensions asking 'What if . . . ?'
- Make and investigate a general statement about familiar numbers or shapes by finding examples that satisfy it.
- Develop from explaining a generalised relationship in words to expressing it in a formula using letters as symbols.

Differentiation

More able: Pupil's Textbook page 38

Average: PCM 12 (same problem, but with less demanding numbers and more guidance). Ideas for predictions are included in **Teacher focus for activity**.

Less able: PCM 12 (same problem as Average; differentiation by outcome)

Introducing the problem

Display a chessboard or an 8×8 chequered grid. Ask children to estimate how many squares are on the grid. Establish that there are more squares than just the 64 small squares. Point out the 2×2, 3×3 . . .

8×8 squares. Explain to children that in this lesson they are going to investigate the number of squares that can be found in square grids of various sizes.

Teacher focus for activity

All children: Encourage children to be systematic when counting squares of each size, by asking questions such as: *How can we make sure that we don't miss out any 2×2 squares, 3×3 squares and so on?* Suggestions might include starting each count at the top left of the grid and counting from left to right, top to bottom, shifting along or down one grid square at a time. Children may find it helpful when counting to use a paper grid and to slide a paper square of each size systematically over its surface.

Point to a sequence of numbers in the table and ask: *Can you see a pattern? What if you look at the differences between consecutive numbers?*

For children who identify square numbers in the table, suggest that they use the index notation [2] to indicate square numbers, as this will help to make patterns clearer.

More able: Encourage children to record their findings clearly so patterns can be seen more easily, e.g. using a table like the one on PCM 12.

Once children have worked out the number of squares in a chessboard, can they describe a way of working out the number of squares in a square grid of any size?

Average: (ideas for predictions) Where appropriate, ask children to make predictions, e.g. *Can you use any of your patterns to predict what would happen with a 6 × 6 grid? Make your prediction then try it. What about a 7 × 7 . . . an 8 × 8 chessboard?*

Optional adult input

Work with the Less able group. Help children to count and record the squares in each grid systematically.

Plenary

Draw the incomplete table from PCM 12 on the board.

1 Invite children to help you complete the table row by row.

grid size	number of					total
	1 × 1 squares	2 × 2 squares	3 × 3 squares	4 × 4 squares	5 × 5 squares	
1 × 1						
2 × 2						
3 × 3						

As the table is completed, ask children if they can identify any patterns. They may notice:

- sequences of square numbers in rows and columns;

- diagonals of repeated numbers;

- a 'shift' relationship between consecutive rows and columns;

- the differences between consecutive numbers in the 'total' column are all square numbers.

You may want to use a different colour to write each table entry using the index notation ^{2} to make patterns clearer.

2 Ask if any children managed to find out how many squares are in an 8 × 8 chessboard and to explain how they did so. Tell children that together you are going to use patterns in the table to see if the answers given are right.

Ask children to predict the numbers for the next 3 rows. These are as follows:

6 × 6:	36	25	16	9	4	1		91
7 × 7:	49	36	25	16	9	4	1	140
8 × 8:	64	49	36	25	16	9	4	1	204

Establish whether given answers for the chessboard are correct (204).

3 Invite children to explain how you could find the total number of squares in a 20 × 20 grid. (Find the total of $20^2 \times 19^2 \times 18^2 \times \ldots \times 1^2$)

Development

Children work out the number of squares in larger grids such as 10 × 10 or even 20 × 20.

Solutions

Textbook page 38
Number of squares on an 8 × 8 chessboard = $8^2 + 7^2 + 6^2 + 5^2 + 4^2 + 3^2 + 2^2 + 1^2 = 204$

PCM 12

grid size	number of					total
	1 × 1 squares	2 × 2 squares	3 × 3 squares	4 × 4 squares	5 × 5 squares	
1 × 1	1	0	0	0	0	1
2 × 2	4	1	0	0	0	5
3 × 3	9	4	1	0	0	14
4 × 4	16	9	4	1	0	30
5 × 5	25	16	9	4	1	55

Description of patterns will vary but should make reference to square numbers. (For examples, see part **1** of the **Plenary**.)

28 Economical boxes

Minimum prior experience

areas of rectangles; properties of cuboids

Resources

Pupil's Textbook page 39, PCM 13, centimetre cubes, centimetre squared paper

Key vocabulary

surface area, centimetre cube, cuboid, factor, factorise, pattern, systematic

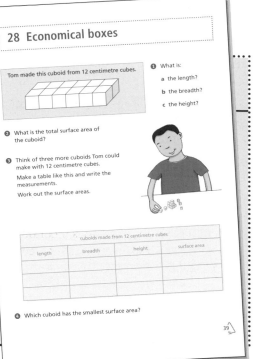

What's the problem?

Investigations of cuboid boxes and surface areas requiring systematic working, reasoning and identification of patterns. They provide opportunities to discuss how to calculate the volume of a cuboid.

Problem solving objectives

- Explain methods and reasoning, orally and in writing.
- Solve mathematical problems or puzzles, recognise and explain patterns and relationships, generalise and predict. Suggest extensions asking 'What if . . .?'

Differentiation

More able: PCM 13 Economical boxes 2

Average: PCM 13 Economical boxes 1 (similar problem, but with fewer possibilities to consider)

Less able: Pupil's Textbook page 39 (similar problem, but with greater structure)

Introducing the problem

Revise the area of rectangles. Establish that the area of a rectangle is the length multiplied by the width (or breadth).

Revise the surface area of cuboids. Establish that the surface area of a cuboid is the sum of the areas of all of its faces.

Discuss the properties of cuboids. Establish, for example, that a cuboid has 6 faces and that opposite faces are identical.

Explain that in this lesson children will be investigating the surface area of cuboids.

Teacher focus for activity

All children: (Children may find it helpful to use centimetre cubes or centimetre squared paper.) Try to elicit from children the need to find factors when investigating the possible dimensions of a cuboid that holds a given number of centimetre cubes. Ask questions such as: *Could one of the measurements be 5 centimetres? Why not? Could one of the measurements be 4 centimetres? How do you know? What else could one of the measurements be?*

Encourage children to investigate dimensions in a systematic way. For example, for a box holding 48 centimetres cubes, starting with dimensions of $1 \text{ cm} \times 1 \text{ cm} \times 48 \text{ cm}$, then $1 \text{ cm} \times 2 \text{ cm} \times 24 \text{ cm}$, then $1 \text{ cm} \times 3 \text{ cm} \times 16 \text{ cm}$, and so on.

More able: Children may not realise that there are choices as to which face is the 'open' face in each cuboid. Ask: *Why have you chosen this face for the opening? What would happen if you chose this one instead?*

Optional adult input

Work with the Less able group. Help children to find the different cuboids and their surface areas, using centimetre cubes if necessary.

Plenary

1 Invite children from each group to give you the dimensions of different cuboids they found. Starting with cuboids with two 1 cm dimensions, establish that they are:

- cuboid holding 12 cubes (Textbook page 39)
  1 cm × 1 cm × 12 cm; 1 cm × 2 cm × 6 cm;
  1 cm × 3 cm × 4 cm; 2 cm × 2 cm × 3cm

- cuboid holding 24 cubes (Economical boxes 1)
  1 cm × 1 cm × 24 cm; 1 cm × 2 cm × 12 cm;
  1 cm × 3 cm × 8 cm; 1 cm × 4 cm × 6 cm;
  2 cm × 2 cm × 6 cm; 2 cm × 3 cm × 4 cm

- cuboid holding 48 cubes (Economical boxes 2)
  1 cm × 1 cm × 48 cm; 1 cm × 2 cm × 24 cm;
  1 cm × 3 cm × 16 cm; 1 cm × 4 cm × 12 cm;
  1 cm × 6 cm × 8 cm; 2 cm × 2 cm × 12 cm;
  2 cm × 3 cm × 8 cm; 2 cm × 4 cm × 6 cm;
  3 cm × 4 cm × 4 cm

2 Discuss with children the different ways in which they found these dimensions. Establish that working out the factors of each number (factorising) is useful. It is also helpful to work systematically. (For more about factors see **Useful mathematical information pages 87–88**.)

3 Invite children who did Economical boxes 1 or Textbook page 39 to say which cuboid has the smallest surface area. Establish that the smallest surface area for the 24-cube cuboid is 52 cm^2 and for the 12-cube cuboid, it is 32 cm^2.

Ask children to explain how they calculated the surface areas of the cuboids.

Establish that, because opposite faces of a cuboid have equal areas, we need only work out the area of 3 faces and double them.

4 Now focus on Economical boxes 2. Invite children to explain how they found the surface area of the open box that uses the least amount of card.

Methods are likely to involve finding all possible cuboids as above and then finding the surface area of each one, but not counting the 'open' face.

Which face is the best one to use as the opening to get the smallest surface area of box? (the largest face)

Finding the total surface area of each cuboid in turn and subtracting the largest face shows that there are two open boxes that use the least amount of card: the 2 cm × 4 cm × 6 cm box with a 4 cm × 6 cm opening and the 3 cm × 4 cm × 4 cm box with a 4 cm × 4 cm opening. Both use 64 cm^2 of card.

Development

Children investigate, in a similar way, boxes that will hold 36 centimetre cubes.

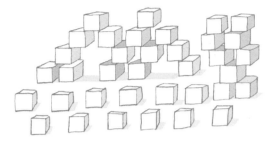

Solutions

Textbook page 39

1 **a** 6 cm   **b** 2 cm   **c** 1 cm
2 40 cm^2
3

cuboids made from 12 centimetre cubes			
length	breadth	height	surface area
12	1	1	50 cm^2
4	3	1	38 cm^2
3	2	2	32 cm^2

(dimensions for each cuboid are interchangeable)

4 3 cm × 2 cm × 2 cm cuboid (surface area 32 cm^2)

PCM 13 Economical boxes 1

4 cm × 3 cm × 2 cm cuboid (dimensions are interchangeable). It uses 52 cm^2 of card.

PCM 13 Economical boxes 2

64 cm^2

29 Investigating diagonals

Minimum prior experience

identifying and continuing number patterns; diagonals; 2-D shapes

Resources

Pupil's Textbook pages 40 and 41, PCM 14, a large hexagon and octagon (regular or irregular)

Key vocabulary

diagonal, polygon, 2-D shape names, pattern, relationship, sequence, formula, rule, predict, triangular number

29 Investigating diagonals

A triangle has no diagonals.

A quadrilateral has 2 diagonals.

① You need PCM 14.

a How many diagonals do these polygons have?

pentagon   hexagon   heptagon

b Copy and complete this table.

number of sides	3	4	5	6	7
number of diagonals					

② Can you see a pattern in the number of diagonals? Try to describe it.

③ Use the pattern to predict how many diagonals these polygons will have:
a an octagon   b a nonagon (9 sides)   c a decagon (10 sides).

40

What's the problem?

Investigating the relationship between the number of diagonals and sides in polygons, identifying and using patterns to make predictions and perhaps to derive a formula.

Problem solving objectives

- Explain methods and reasoning, orally and in writing.
- Solve mathematical problems or puzzles, recognise and explain patterns and relationships, generalise and predict. Suggest extensions asking 'What if . . . ?'
- Make and investigate a general statement about familiar numbers or shapes by finding examples that satisfy it.
- Develop from explaining a generalised relationship in words to expressing it in a formula using letters as symbols.

Differentiation

More able: Pupil's Textbook page 41, questions 4 to 6

Average: Pupil's Textbook page 40, questions 1 to 3 (same problem, but with greater guidance and less demanding predictions). Children could move on to question 5.

Less able: Pupil's Textbook page 40, questions 1 to 3 (same problem as Average, differentiation by outcome)

Introducing the problem

Establish the meaning of 'diagonal' (a straight line joining 2 non-adjacent vertices of a polygon). Invite children to tell you the number of diagonals in a quadrilateral (2). Confirm this by drawing a variety of quadrilaterals on the board and inviting children to draw on the diagonals.

How many diagonals does a triangle have? (none)

Ask children to predict how many diagonals a pentagon has. Do not confirm their answers. Explain that in this lesson they will be investigating the numbers of diagonals in different polygons.

Teacher focus on activity

All children: Encourage children to draw diagonals systematically. *How can we make sure we don't miss any diagonals?* Elicit that drawing **all** the diagonals from one vertex before dealing with the next, will help. It will also give children a 'feel' for pattern.

When children are trying to establish a pattern in the ordered number of diagonals, you may need to prompt them into finding the difference between consecutive numbers.

More able: Encourage children to record their results in an ordered way. Prompt children trying to generalise to investigate the relationship between the number of diagonals at each vertex of a shape and the number of sides (see **Useful mathematical information page 88**).

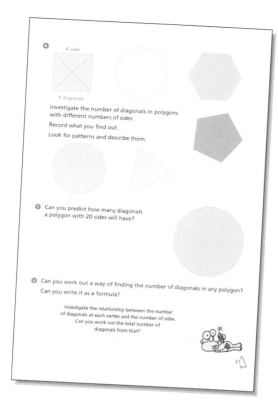

4 sides

2 diagonals

Investigate the number of diagonals in polygons with different numbers of sides.
Record what you find out.
Look for patterns and describe them.

⑤ Can you predict how many diagonals a polygon with 20 sides will have?

⑥ Can you work out a way of finding the number of diagonals in any polygon?
Can you write it as a formula?

Investigate the relationship between the number of diagonals at each vertex and the number of sides.
Can you work out the total number of diagonals from that?

41

Optional adult input

Work with the Average and Less able groups. Help children to develop a systematic way of drawing and counting diagonals.

Plenary

Display a large hexagon and octagon on which diagonals can be drawn.

1 Invite children from the Average group to describe their investigation, using the shapes for illustration. Help other children to understand the explanations and encourage them to ask questions.

Discuss the methods of investigation in terms of how systematic they are. Involve all children, e.g. *Who else got the same result? Who else got a pattern of numbers like this? What do you think he/she did next? What do you think the next result is?*

At some point complete this table together:

number of sides	3	4	5	6	7
number of diagonals	0	2	5	9	14

Point out that recording in a table makes it easier to identify patterns and relationships.

Invite children to describe the pattern in the bottom row. Establish that the difference between consecutive numbers increases by 1 each time. Some children may also notice that each number is a triangular number minus 1. (See **Useful mathematical information pages 82–83** for more about triangular numbers.)

Invite children to predict the number of diagonals for shapes with 8, 9, 10, 11 . . . sides.

2 *Has anybody worked out a way of predicting the number of diagonals for a polygon with any number of sides?* Methods are likely to be along the following lines: Multiply the number of sides by the number of sides minus 3 and then divide by 2.

Ask children to explain how they worked this out (see **Useful mathematical information page 88**). Get children to test the method on a triangle and a square. Then use the method to calculate the number of diagonals in shapes with 50 sides and 100 sides.

Invite children to express the method as a formula, e.g. $D = (S \times (S - 3)) \div 2$, where D = number of diagonals and S = number of sides.

Development

Children investigate shapes formed within regular polygons in which all the diagonals have been drawn.

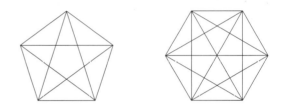

Solutions

1 a pentagon: 5 diagonals; hexagon: 9 diagonals; heptagon: 14 diagonals

b See table in **Plenary**

2 The difference between consecutive numbers of diagonals increases by 1 each time.

3 a octagon: 20 diagonals

b nonagon: 27 diagonals

c decagon: 35 diagonals

4 Children's own findings and explanations – likely to be similar to the solutions for questions **1** to **3**.

5 170 diagonals

6 The number of diagonals for any polygon could be worked out as follows:
Multiply the number of sides by the number of sides minus 3 and then divide by 2.
Formula: $D = (S \times (S - 3)) \div 2$, where D = number of diagonals and S = number of sides.

30 Magic shapes

Minimum prior experience

mental addition and subtraction of several 1- or 2-digit numbers; relationship between addition and subtraction

Resources

PCMs 15 and 16 (plus extra copies), an enlarged copy of the star on PCM 15, scrap paper

Key vocabulary

sum, difference, total, strategy, method, trial and improvement

What's the problem?

Number puzzles involving reasoning about numbers, an ability to add several numbers mentally, systematic working and an understanding of the relationship between addition and subtraction.

Problem solving objective

- Solve mathematical problems or puzzles, recognise and explain patterns and relationships, generalise and predict. Suggest extensions asking 'What if . . . ?'

Differentiation

Puzzles can be simplified by inserting more numbers before PCMs are copied (see **Solutions**).

More able: PCM 16 Magic shapes 3

Average: PCM 15 Magic shapes 2 (similar problem, but with less demanding numbers)

Less able: PCM 15 Magic shapes 1 (similar problem, but using a less demanding arrangement)

Introducing the problem

Explain to children that in this lesson they will be solving number puzzles involving addition and subtraction. Advise them to work in an ordered and neat way, otherwise it may be difficult for them to keep track of what they have done.

Teacher focus for activity

All children: Discuss with children ordered ways of working, e.g. ways of keeping track of numbers that are possibilities and numbers that have been tried and eliminated.

Ask questions that will help children to reason about the numbers, e.g. *What do those 2 numbers add up to? So what do those 2 numbers need to add up to? What are the possibilities? Why can't these 2 numbers go in the circles?*

Some children may find it helpful to systematically list combinations of 3 or 4 numbers with the given total.

Use your discretion as to whether and when to help children by inserting additional numbers for them.

Less able: Children who manage to solve the problem could try Magic shapes 2 with more numbers pre-inserted.

Optional adult input

Work with the Average group using the questions suggested above.

Plenary

Display a large version of the star on PCM 15 and list the numbers 1 to 12.

Cross out the numbers 1, 2, 3 and 4 from the list.

1 Ask children to suggest ways in which to work through the puzzle.

As the puzzle is worked through, encourage children to reason about numbers by asking questions such as: *What must the sum of the numbers be? What could the numbers be? What are all the possibilities? Why couldn't that be one of the numbers?* One possible path of reasoning is as follows:

- Start with the line containing 1 and 2.
  The missing two numbers must add up to 23 as the total for the line is 26.
  The only pair of numbers with a total of 23 is 11 and 12.
  So pencil in the possibilities of 11 or 12 by each circle.
  Cross out 11 and 12 from the list.

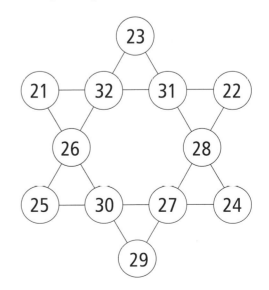

- Consider the line containing 3 and 4.
  The sum of the missing numbers must be 19.
  If one of the numbers is the pencilled-in 11 then the other number must be 8.
  If one of the numbers is the pencilled-in 12 then the other number must be 7.
  Pencil in 7 and 8.

  And so on.

As the puzzle is worked through, pencilled-in numbers can be confirmed or discarded and crossed out in the list until all numbers have been correctly placed.

Explain that this method of solving a problem is known as 'trial and improvement'.

2 Another possible method involves systematically listing all combinations of four numbers with a total of 26: 1, 2, 11, 12; 1, 3, 10, 12; 1, 4, 9, 12; 1, 4, 10, 11; 1, 5, 8, 12 . . . Although a lengthy process to start with, the combinations can be used to solve the puzzle in minutes.

Development

Ask: *Can you solve your problem in a different way, starting with a blank diagram?*

Solutions

PCM 15 Magic shapes 1

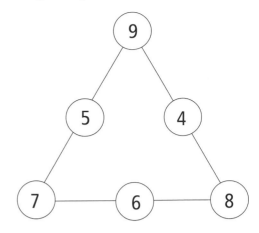

PCM 15 Magic shapes 2

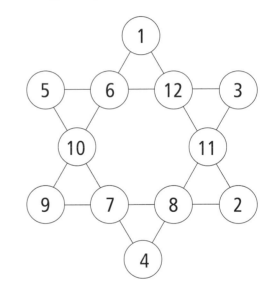

PCM 16, Magic shapes 3

Useful mathematical information

These pages provide further explanation of the mathematics used in some lessons. Each section is referenced to the relevant activity so that it is easy to find what is needed starting from the lesson plan for the problem.

Some sections cover the mathematics that underpins the problem. Other sections cover specific mathematical concepts that children will need to understand. Both are intended to be information for the non-specialist mathematics teacher.

An algebraic approach to Cycle tour

(Lesson 1)

If F is the distance travelled on the first day then the total distance travelled in the 9 days can be represented by:

$$F + (F - 6) + (F - 12) + (F - 18) + (F - 24) + (F - 30) + (F - 36) + (F - 42) + (F - 48) = 315$$

Simplifying, we get:

$9F - 216 = 315$

so, $9F = 315 + 216 = 531$

so, $F = 531 \div 9 = 59$

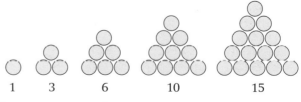

The distance travelled on the first day is 59 miles.

Methods of long division

(Lessons 1, 6 and 19)

Here are 3 possible approaches to the division of large numbers. These methods could be used mentally with informal written jottings for numbers of any size.

- Finding out how many times the divisor can be subtracted from the number using multiples of the divisor.

For example, for 5126 ÷ 24:

```
  5126
– 2400          100 × 24
  2726
– 2400          100 × 24
   326
–  240           10 × 24
    86
–   72            3 × 24
    14          Answer: 213 remainder 14
```

- Using a standard written method of division. For example, for 5126 ÷ 24:

```
      213
  24)5126
     48
     32
     24
     86
     72
     14          Answer: 213 remainder 14
```

- Using an informal 'building up' method. For example, for 2000 ÷ 60:

  I know 10 × 60 = 600.
  3 lots of 600 make 1800, so 30 × 60 = 1800
  I've got another 200 to go to get to 2000.
  3 × 60 = 180, so that's all the 60s that will fit and there's 20 left to go.
  So 2000 ÷ 60 = 33 remainder 20

Triangular numbers

(Lessons 2, 15, 24 and 29)

Triangular numbers are the numbers generated by dots arranged in the form of a sequence of growing triangles.

```
  1      3      6      10      15
```

The sequence continues 21, 28, 36, 45 . . .

The difference between one triangular number and the next increases by one each time.

triangular numbers   1   3   6   10   15 ...

difference   2   3   4   5 ...

The sequence of triangular numbers frequently occurs in mathematics, particularly in investigations of patterns.

Grid method of multiplication

(Lessons 6 and 13)

The grid method of multiplication involves decomposing each number into its place value components and multiplying every component in one number by every component in the other and adding the results. For example, 127×36:

×	100	20	7
30	3000	600	210
6	600	120	42

$\Rightarrow$ 3810
$\Rightarrow$ +   762
        4572

So, $127 \times 36 = 4572$

Order of operations in a number sentence

(Lesson 8)

In a number sentence, brackets indicate that the contents are to be treated as a unit and, usually, evaluated first. For example, in the following expression 6 and 2 are added first and the result is multiplied by 5:

$(6 + 2) \times 5 = 40$

However in the following expression, the product of 2 and 5 is found first and then added to 6:

$6 + (2 \times 5) = 16$

It is the mathematical convention that once the operations within brackets have been carried out, then divisions and multiplications from left to right take priority, followed by additions and subtractions. This can be remembered by the acronym BoDMAS (Brackets over Division, Multiplication, Addition, Subtraction).

So even without the brackets the answer to $6 + 2 \times 5$ is 16.

Calculators used in primary classrooms are usually 'simple' or 'arithmetic'. They do not apply the BoDMAS convention and merely carry out operations in the order in which they are input. The result of inputting $6 + 2 \times 5$ in a simple calculator would result in 40, the wrong answer. With scientific calculators, on the other hand, it is possible to input brackets and also, the BoDMAS convention is applied.

Dotty polygons

(Lesson 9)

Is there a limit to the number of dots that a polygon with 12 perimeter dots can have inside it?

A line can be drawn from one dot to any dot in an adjacent row or column, however far away the second dot is, without intersecting any other dots. So a line that is infinitely long can be drawn from one dot to another without intersecting any other dots.

It is possible to have all the 12 adjacent perimeter dots in adjacent columns or rows. It is therefore possible to have a 12 perimeter-dot polygon with infinitely long sides. If there is no limit to the length of the sides of the polygon, there is no limit to the size of the polygon and therefore no limit to the number of dots that can be contained within it.

Adding fractions

(Lesson 10)

To add (or subtract) fractions they must be converted to equivalent fractions with a common denominator. Sometimes this is relatively simple, e.g. to add $\frac{1}{3}$ and $\frac{1}{6}$ we can convert $\frac{1}{3}$ to $\frac{2}{6}$ and then add: $\frac{2}{6} + \frac{1}{6} = \frac{3}{6} (= \frac{1}{2})$. We can use a fraction 'wall' to demonstrate this.

1 whole					
$\frac{1}{3}$		$\frac{1}{3}$		$\frac{1}{3}$	
$\frac{1}{6}$	$\frac{1}{6}$	$\frac{1}{6}$	$\frac{1}{6}$	$\frac{1}{6}$	$\frac{1}{6}$

Sometimes, a suitable common denominator is not so obvious, e.g. with $\frac{1}{3}$, $\frac{1}{4}$ and $\frac{1}{5}$. In such cases we need to find a number that is a multiple of all the denominators (a number that they will all divide into).

The lowest common multiple of the denominators of $\frac{1}{3}$, $\frac{1}{4}$ and $\frac{1}{5}$ is 60. This means that we can convert each fraction into sixtieths.

At this stage we need to remember that multiplying (or dividing) the numerator and denominator of a fraction by the same number produces an equivalent fraction.

To change $\frac{1}{3}$ to sixtieths we need to multiply the denominator (3) by 20. So we must also multiply the numerator by 20:

$$\frac{1}{3} \xrightarrow{(\times 20)} \frac{20}{60}$$

Similarly, to change $\frac{1}{4}$ to sixtieths, we need to multiply denominator and numerator by 15:

$$\frac{1}{4} \xrightarrow{(\times 15)} \frac{15}{60}$$

To change $\frac{1}{5}$ to sixtieths we must multiply denominator and numerator by 12:

$$\frac{1}{5} \xrightarrow{(\times 12)} \frac{12}{60}$$

So $\frac{1}{3} + \frac{1}{4} + \frac{1}{5} = \frac{20}{60} + \frac{15}{60} + \frac{12}{60} = \frac{47}{60}$

Equal numbers of 10p and 5p stamps in Stamps

(Lesson 11)

10p	5p	50p	value
1	1	98	£49.15
2	2	96	£48.30
3	3	94	£47.45
4	4	92	£46.60

This table shows combinations of stamps where there is an equal number of 10p and 5p stamps. There are several ways of determining whether or not a total of £10 can be achieved using this combination of stamps. Here are two:

- The value of the stamps decreases by 85p in each row. If we repeatedly subtract 85p from £49.15, we can determine if one of the results is £10. A quicker way of finding this out is to see if the difference between £49.15 and £10 is divisible by 85p.

  £49.15 − £10 = £39.15

  3915p ÷ 85p = 46.0588 . . .

Clearly the difference between £49.15 and £10 is not divisible by 85p, so a value of £10 is not achievable where there is an equal number of 10p and 5p stamps.

- A whole number of pounds can be achieved only in rows where there is an even number of 5p (and 10p) stamps – otherwise values would end with 5p. The value of the 50p stamps in an 'even' row will always be a whole number of pounds. So if the total value of the row is to be a whole number of pounds then the sum of the 10p and 5p stamps must be a multiple of a pound in an even row. This will only occur when the number of 5p stamps is a multiple of 20.

In row 20, the stamps' value would be:
(10p × 20) + (5p × 20) + (50p × 60) = £30

In row 40, the stamps' value would be:
(10p × 40) + (5p × 40) + (50p × 20) = £16

In row 60, the total number of stamps would exceed 100.

So a value of £10 is not achievable where there is an equal number of 10p and 5p stamps.

Leap years

(Lesson 13)

A year is the length of time it takes the Earth to complete one orbit of the Sun. This is approximately $365\frac{1}{4}$ days. For convenience, we count a year as 365 days and account for the extra quarter by having a leap year with 366 days every fourth year.

So, as a general rule, a leap year is a year that is divisible by 4, but there are exceptions (because the orbit is not exactly $365\frac{1}{4}$ days). Years that are multiples of 100, but are not multiples of 400, are not leap years.

For example:

The year 2008 is a leap year because it is divisible by 4.

The year 2100 is not a leap year, because although it is divisible by 4, it is also a multiple of 100 that is not a multiple of 400.

The year 2000 is a leap year because it is divisible by 4 and although it is a multiple of 100 it is also a multiple of 400.

Incidentally, if the last 2 digits of a year are divisible by 4, then the whole year is divisible by 4 (see 'Factors and rules of divisibility' on page 87).

Difference between mass and weight

(Lesson 14)

Mass is a measure of the quantity of matter in an object and is constant. Weight is the measure of the gravitational pull on an object and can vary, depending upon which part of the world, or on which planet, the object is. In science, the distinction is important; in everyday usage the term 'weight' is used regardless.

In **Personal weights**, the Hoskins family, by using compression scales, are actually finding their weights. If they took the same scales to the moon and weighed themselves, because the gravitational pull is less, their weights would be less.

Alternative reasoning for Personal weights

(Lesson 14)

Add the results of these weighings:

Mr and Mrs Hoskins	155 kg
Mrs Hoskins and Mat	147 kg
Mr Hoskins and Mat	152 kg
Total	454 kg

Because Mr and Mrs Hoskins and Mat are each included twice in these weighings, the answer represents twice their total weight. Dividing by 2 will give the total weight of Mr and Mrs Hoskins and Mat.

So Mr Hoskins and Mrs Hoskins and Mat altogether weigh 454 kg ÷ 2 = 227 kg

We know that Mr and Mrs Hoskins weigh 155 kg together, so if we subtract this weight from 227 kg, we are left with:

Mat's weight = 227 kg − 155 kg = 72 kg

We can now subtract Mat's weight from the other combined weights to find the weights of each of the other family members.

An alternative approach to School disco

(Lesson 17)

Fractions could be used to a greater or lesser extent in all of the problems, e.g.

$\frac{1}{2}$ of all the children remained after 8:00
$\frac{1}{2}$ of $\frac{1}{2}$ or $\frac{1}{4}$ of all the children remained after 8:30
$\frac{1}{2}$ of $\frac{1}{4}$ or $\frac{1}{8}$ of all the children remained after 9:00
30 children remained after 9:00
So $\frac{1}{8}$ of all the children = 30 children
So all the children = 30 × 8 = 240 children

Finding 5000 days after the start of this year

(Lesson 19)

Here are 2 strategies for finding the solution. There are many possible variations.

- Strategy 1

    Assume there are 365 days in each year. Calculate the number of years there are in 5000 days, by finding 5000 ÷ 365. (13 ordinary years and 255 days – see below.)

> 5000 ÷ 365 can be calculated in various ways. Here are two possible methods:
> - Repeated subtraction
>
> $$\begin{array}{r} 5000 \\ -\ 3650 \quad (365 \times 10) \\ \hline 1350 \\ -\ 1095 \quad (365 \times 3) \\ \hline \end{array}$$
>
>   255 days remaining, so 5000 days is 13 ordinary years and 255 days
> - Using a calculator
>
>   5000 ÷ 365 = 13.69863
>
>   This tells us that in 5000 days there are 13 whole years and a fraction of a year.
>
>   13 whole years = 365 × 13 = 4745 days
>
>   5000 − 4745 = 255 days, so 5000 days is 13 ordinary years and 255 days

Successively subtract the number of days in each month in the 14th (partial) year from the number of remaining days as far as possible:

$$
\begin{array}{rl}
255 & \\
-\;31 & \text{(January)} \\
\hline
224 & \\
-\;28 & \text{(February)} \\
\hline
196 & \\
-\;31 & \text{(March)} \\
\hline
165 & \\
-\;30 & \text{(April)} \\
\hline
135 & \\
-\;31 & \text{(May)} \\
\hline
104 & \\
-\;30 & \text{(June)} \\
\hline
74 & \\
-\;31 & \text{(July)} \\
\hline
43 & \\
-\;31 & \text{(August)} \\
\hline
12 & \text{(days of September)}
\end{array}
$$

This takes us 12 days into September, i.e. to midnight on the 12th September.

Adjust the result to take account of leap years. In the 14 years (including the partial year) there will be either 3 or 4 leap years (see page 84 for more about leap years). For each leap year, the 5000 days will be completed one day earlier.

So, the time will be 12 midnight on 9th September (with 3 leap years) or 8th September (with 4 leap years) in the 14th year after the start of the current year.

- Strategy 2

  Successively subtract the number of days in a year from 5000 days as far as possible, taking account of leap years as they occur.

  In the example below, the first leap year to occur is the 2nd year.

$$
\begin{array}{rl}
5000 & \\
-\;\;\;365 & \text{(1 normal year)} \\
\hline
4635 & \\
-\;\;\;366 & \text{(1 leap year)} \\
\hline
4269 & \\
-\;1095 & \text{(3 normal years)} \\
\hline
3174 & \\
-\;\;\;366 & \text{(1 leap year)} \\
\hline
2808 & \\
-\;1095 & \text{(3 normal years)} \\
\hline
1713 & \\
-\;\;\;366 & \text{(1 leap year)} \\
\hline
1347 & \\
-\;1095 & \text{(3 normal years)} \\
\hline
252 & \text{days remaining}
\end{array}
$$

5000 days is 13 years and 252 days in the 14th year.

Successively subtract the number of days in each month in the 14th (partial) year from the number of remaining days as far as possible. This step is essentially the same as in Strategy 1 except that if the 14th year is a leap year then 29 days are subtracted for February.

The time arrived at will be 12 midnight on 9th September (with 3 leap years) or 8th September (with 4 leap years) in the 14th year after the start of the current year.

The total number of slabs in Patio patterns

(Lesson 20)

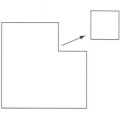

arm length	2	3	4	5	6
total number of slabs	15	21	27	33	39

We can view each patio as a square with a square corner removed.

We can find the total number of slabs (T) in the patio by subtracting the number of slabs in the small corner square from the number of slabs in the big square.

It can be seen from the patio pictures that the length of the big square is always 2 more than the length of the arm ($L + 2$).

So the number of slabs in the big square must be
$(L + 2) \times (L + 2)$ or $(L + 2)^2$

It can also be seen that the length of the small square is always one less than the arm length ($L - 1$).

So the number of slabs in the small square must be
$(L - 1) \times (L - 1)$ or $(L - 1)^2$

Subtracting one from the other gives:
$T = (L + 2)^2 - (L - 1)^2$

The value of L can be substituted into this formula directly.

The formula, simplified algebraically, is $T = 6L + 3$, where T is the total number of slabs and L is the arm length of the red ∟ shape.

This simplified formula can be derived directly from the table.

> Simplifying $T = (L + 2)^2 - (L - 1)^2$ algebraically (for your interest only – children would not need to do this):
>
> $$\begin{aligned} T &= (L + 2)^2 - (L - 1)^2 \\ &= (L^2 + 4L + 4) - (L^2 - 2L + 1) \\ &= L^2 + 4L + 4 - L^2 + 2L - 1 \\ &= 6L + 3 \end{aligned}$$

Percentages

(Lesson 22)

Per cent means 'out of one hundred'. Percentages are essentially fractions with 100 as the denominator. So $36\% = \frac{36}{100}$; $99\% = \frac{99}{100}$.

To calculate common percentages such as 50%, 25%, 75%, 10% and 20%, it is useful to know their fractional equivalents:

$50\% = \frac{50}{100} = \frac{1}{2}$;　$25\% = \frac{25}{100} = \frac{1}{4}$;　$75\% = \frac{75}{100} = \frac{3}{4}$;

$10\% = \frac{10}{100} = \frac{1}{10}$;　$20\% = \frac{20}{100} = \frac{2}{10}$ or $\frac{1}{5}$

Fractions for other multiples of 10% can be derived from the fractions for 10% and 20%:

$30\% = \frac{3}{10}$;　$40\% = \frac{4}{10}$ or $\frac{2}{5}$;　$60\% = \frac{6}{10}$ or $\frac{3}{5}$

Once the fractional equivalent of a percentage is known then percentages of quantities can be found, e.g.

- 10% of £30 is equivalent to $\frac{1}{10}$ of £30.
  $\frac{1}{10}$ of £30 = £30 ÷ 10 = £3
  So 10% of £30 is £3.

- 70% of £50 = $\frac{7}{10}$ of £50.
  $\frac{1}{10}$ of £50 = £5, so $\frac{7}{10}$ of £50 = £5 × 7 = £35
  So 70% of £50 is £35.

- 20% of £15 = $\frac{1}{5}$ of £15 = £15 ÷ 5 = £3
  So 20% of £15 is £3.

- $12\frac{1}{2}\%$ of £40 is half of 25% of £40.
  25% of £40 is $\frac{1}{4}$ of £40 = £10
  So $12\frac{1}{2}\%$ of £40 = $\frac{1}{2}$ of £10 = £5
  So $12\frac{1}{2}\%$ of £40 is £5.

Deriving the formula for Handshakes

(Lesson 24)

- Method 1
  Because nobody shakes hands with themselves, it can be reasoned that each person shakes hands with one less than the total number of people ($P - 1$ handshakes, where P is the number of people).

  For everybody, that would be $P \times (P - 1)$, except that each handshake is shared by 2 people.

  So $H = (P \times (P - 1)) \div 2$, where H is the total number of handshakes.

  (Compare this formula with the formula derived in **29 Investigating diagonals**.)

- Method 2
  Another approach is to establish a relationship between the numbers in the top row and the numbers in the bottom row of the table.

number of people	1	2	3	4	5	6	7
number of handshakes	0	1	3	6	10	15	21

1	2		2	3		3	4		4	5		5	6		6	7
1				3			6			10			15			21

Focusing on various inverted 'L' shapes in the table we can see that the bottom number in the inverted 'L' is half the product of the 2 upper numbers. In other words, the number of handshakes for any number of people is half the product of the number of people and the number of people minus 1 or, symbolically:

$H = (P \times (P - 1)) \div 2$, where H is the number of handshakes and P is the number of people.

Factors and rules of divisibility

(Lesson 28)

The factors of a number are those numbers that will divide into it exactly, including 1 and the number itself, e.g. the factors of 6 are 1, 2, 3 and 6. The most efficient approach for finding all the factors of a number is to test the number for divisibility by each number starting with 2. Factors are usually found in pairs.

For example finding the factors of 48:
all whole numbers are divisible
by 1 and themselves   1, 48

48 is divisible by 2.	$2 \times 24 = 48$ so 2 and 24 are factors of 48	2, 24
48 is divisible by 3.	$3 \times 16 = 48$ so 3 and 16 are factors of 48	3, 16
48 is divisible by 4.	$4 \times 12 = 48$ so 4 and 12 are factors of 48	4, 12

48 is not divisible by 5.

| 48 is divisible by 6. | $6 \times 8 = 48$, so 6 and 8 are factors of 48 | 6, 8 |

48 is not divisible by 7.

| 48 is divisible by 8. | $8 \times 6 = 48$. We have already listed 6 and 8 | |

From this point on there will be no new factors.

So the factors of 48 are 1, 2, 3, 4, 6, 8, 12, 16, 24, 48.

Rules of divisibility are helpful in finding factors.
For instance, a whole number is divisible by:

- 2 if the units digit is even;
- 3 if the sum of the digits of the number is divisible by 3, e.g. 48 is divisible by 3 because $4 + 8 = 12$ which is divisible by 3;
- 4 if the last two digits are divisible by 4;
- 5 if the units digit is 0 or 5;
- 6 if the number is divisible by 2 and 3 (so an even number for which the sum of the digits is divisible by 3);
- 9 if the sum of the digits is divisible by 9, e.g. 594 is divisible by 9 because $5 + 9 + 4 = 18$, which is divisible by 9;
- 10 if the units digit is 0.

Deriving a formula for Investigating diagonals

(Lesson 29)

The relationship between the number of sides and the number of diagonals is not easy to work out from the table on page 79. It is best worked out through a combination of looking at each polygon in turn, counting the diagonals at each vertex, and reasoning as follows.

Since a vertex cannot be joined by a diagonal to itself, nor to the 2 adjacent vertices, the number of diagonals that can be drawn from one vertex will be 3 less than the number of vertices (or sides).

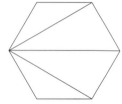

Symbolically, this can be represented by $D = S - 3$, where D is the number of diagonals and S is the number of sides.

It would be wrong to conclude, though, that multiplying the number of diagonals from one vertex by the number of vertices will give the total number of diagonals. It needs to be remembered that each diagonal is 'shared' by 2 vertices, so we need to divide by 2.

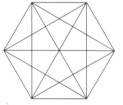

So the number of diagonals in a polygon is found by multiplying the number of sides by the number of sides minus 3 and then dividing by 2.

As a formula, this is:
   $D = (S \times (S - 3)) \div 2$, where D is the number of diagonals and S is the number of sides.

(Compare this formula with the formula derived in **24 Handshakes**.)

Dartboards 1

Paksha has a toy dartboard game.

There are 3 rings with a number in each ring.

You throw 3 darts to make a score.

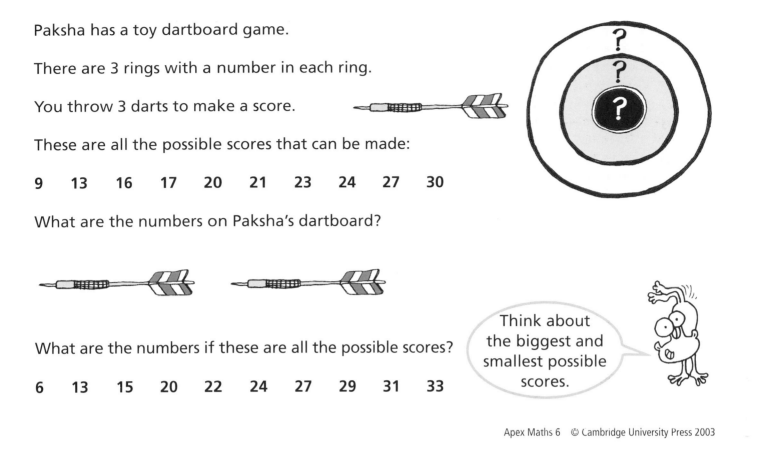

These are all the possible scores that can be made:

9   13   16   17   20   21   23   24   27   30

What are the numbers on Paksha's dartboard?

What are the numbers if these are all the possible scores?

6   13   15   20   22   24   27   29   31   33

Think about the biggest and smallest possible scores.

Apex Maths 6   © Cambridge University Press 2003

Dartboards 2

Paksha has a toy dartboard game.

There are 3 rings with a number in each ring.

You throw 3 darts to make a score.

These are all the possible scores that can be made:

9   13   16   17   20   21   23   24   27   30

What are the numbers on Paksha's dartboard?

What are the numbers if these are all the possible scores?

6   13   15   20   22   24   27   29   31   33

Apex Maths 6   © Cambridge University Press 2003

Magic squares

This is a magic square.

The totals for each row, column and diagonal are the same.

In this square the magic total is 12.

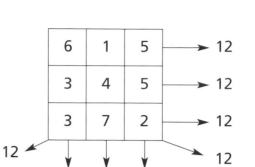

Fill in the missing numbers in these magic squares.

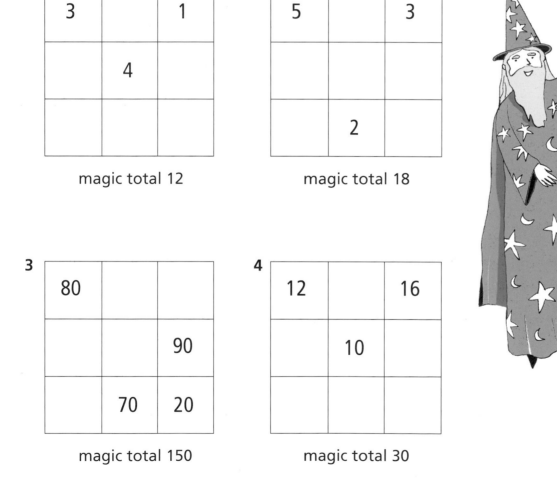

1

3		1
	4	

magic total 12

2

5		3
	2	

magic total 18

3

80		
		90
	70	20

magic total 150

4

12		16
	10	

magic total 30

5 Multiply the numbers in any magic square by 2 to make a new square.

Is the square still magic?

Marco's pizzeria

In Marco's pizzeria each table has a number.

When you have eaten your food you get a bill.

Look at these bills.

Table 1

3 pizzas
1 cola

Total: £11

Table 2

2 Salads
1 pizza
2 colas

Total: £8.50

Table 3

3 Pizzas
4 Colas

Total: £12.50

Table 4

2 pizzas
2 Salads
2 colas

Total:

Work out the total cost of the bill for **Table 4**.

Apex Maths 6 © Cambridge University Press 2003

Marco's pizzeria: Clue 1

Look at the bills for **Tables 1** and **3**.

What is the difference in what was ordered?

What is the difference in price?

Can you work out the cost of one of the items now?

Can you work out the cost of the other item?

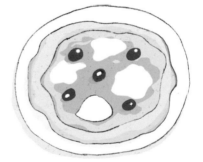

Apex Maths 6   © Cambridge University Press 2003

Marco's pizzeria: Clue 2

Look at the bill for **Table 2**.

Can you work out the cost of another item?

Now you are able to work out the bill for **Table 4**.

Apex Maths 6   © Cambridge University Press 2003

Dotty polygons

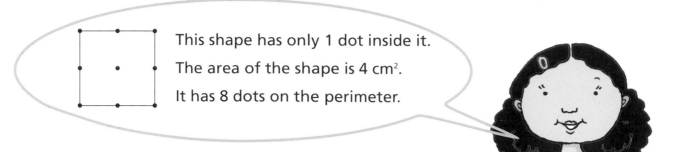

This shape has only 1 dot inside it.

The area of the shape is 4 cm².

It has 8 dots on the perimeter.

These shapes have only 1 dot inside.

Underneath each shape write the area **(a)** and the number of perimeter dots **(b)**.

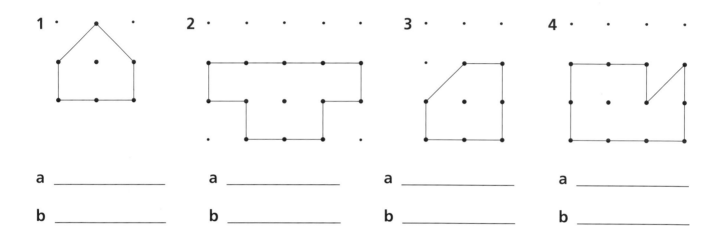

1

a _____

b _____

2

a _____

b _____

3

a _____

b _____

4

a _____

b _____

Draw your own shapes that have only one dot inside.

Write the area and the number of perimeter dots underneath.

Can you see a relationship between the area and the number of perimeter dots?

_____

_____

Fractions challenge 1

When she died, a woman left a pot of gold coins for her children, Jake, Jill and Jo.
Jake got one sixth of the coins.   Jill got one third of the coins.   Jo got 3 coins.

$$\frac{1}{6}$$

Jake

$$\frac{1}{3}$$

Jill

Jo

How many coins did Jill get?

What fraction of the coins did Jake and Jill get between them?

Apex Maths 6   © Cambridge University Press 2003

Fractions challenge 2

When she died, a woman left a pot of gold coins for her children:
Mindy, Mandy, Mog and Meg.

Mindy got one quarter of the coins.   Mandy got one sixth of the coins.

Mog got one twelfth of the coins.   Meg got 6 coins.

How many coins did Mog get?

Apex Maths 6   © Cambridge University Press 2003

Fractions challenge 3

When she died, a woman left a pot of gold coins for her children:
Sindy, Sandy, Sue and Seth.

Sindy got one third of the coins.   Sandy got one quarter of the coins.

Sue got one fifth of the coins.   Seth got 13 coins.

How many coins did Sandy get?

Apex Maths 6   © Cambridge University Press 2003

Personal weights 1

The Hoskins family live on a farm.

They want to weigh themselves.

The only scales they have are old ones used for weighing sheep.

The scales won't weigh anything under 100 kg.

So the family get on the scales 2 at a time.

Mrs Hoskins and her son Mat weigh 147 kg altogether.

Mr and Mrs Hoskins weigh 155 kg altogether.

Mr Hoskins and Mat weigh 152 kg altogether.

What does each member of the family weigh?

Apex Maths 6   © Cambridge University Press 2003

Personal weights 2

The Hoskins family live on a farm.

They want to weigh themselves.

The only scales they have are old ones used for weighing sheep.

The scales won't weigh anything under 100 kg.

So the family get on the scales 2 at a time.

Mr Hoskins and his son Mat weigh 152 kg altogether.

Mr and Mrs Hoskins weigh 155 kg altogether.

Mat and his sister Sally weigh 142 kg altogether.

Mrs Hoskins and Mat weigh 147 kg altogether.

What does each member of the family weigh?

Apex Maths 6   © Cambridge University Press 2003

School disco 1

At the school disco, half the children went home at 8:00 pm.

Half the remaining children went home at 8:30 pm.

Half the remaining children went home at 9:00 pm.

Then there were 30 children left.

How many children were there at the start of the disco?

School disco 2

At the school disco, half the children left at 8:00 pm.

Half the remaining children left at 8:30 pm.

Half the remaining children left at 9:00 pm.

One third of the remaining children stayed to the end at 9:30 pm.

At 9:30 pm there were 10 children.

How many children were there at the start of the disco?

Window investigations 1

Investigate number relationships inside 3 × 3 square windows on a 100 square.

Investigate opposite numbers.
Investigate the centre number.
Try multiplying numbers.
Try adding numbers.

Can you make any general statements?

Investigate other windows.

Try different sized squares.

Try rectangular windows.

Investigate crosses.

1	2	3	4	5	6	7	8	9	10
11	12	13	14	15	16	17	18	19	20
21	22	23	24	25	26	27	28	29	30
31	32	33	34	35	36	37	38	39	40
41	42	43	44	45	46	47	48	49	50
51	52	53	54	55	56	57	58	59	60
61	62	63	64	65	66	67	68	69	70
71	72	73	74	75	76	77	78	79	80
81	82	83	84	85	86	87	88	89	90
91	92	93	94	95	96	97	98	99	100

15	16	17	18	19
25	26	27	28	29
35	36	37	38	39
45	46	47	48	49
55	56	57	58	59

21	22	23	24
31	32	33	34
41	42	43	44

	55	
64	65	66
	75	

Can you make any general statements about the numbers in each shape?

Apex Maths 6   © Cambridge University Press 2003

Window investigations 2

Investigate number relationships inside 3 × 3 square windows on a multiplication square.

Investigate opposite numbers.
Investigate the centre number.
Try multiplying numbers.
Try adding numbers.

Can you make any general statements?

Try different sized squares.
Try rectangular windows.
Investigate crosses.

x	1	2	3	4	5	6	7	8	9	10
1	1	2	3	4	5	6	7	8	9	10
2	2	4	6	8	10	12	14	16	18	20
3	3	6	9	12	15	18	21	24	27	30
4	4	8	12	16	20	24	28	32	36	40
5	5	10	15	20	25	30	35	40	45	50
6	6	12	18	24	30	36	42	48	54	60
7	7	14	21	28	35	42	49	56	63	70
8	8	16	24	32	40	48	56	64	72	80
9	9	18	27	36	45	54	63	72	81	90
10	10	20	30	40	50	60	70	80	90	100

15	20	25	30	35
18	24	30	36	42
21	28	35	42	49
24	32	40	48	56
27	36	45	54	63

21	28	35	42
24	32	40	48
27	36	45	54

	30	
28	35	42
	40	

Investigate other windows.

Apex Maths 6   © Cambridge University Press 2003

100 square

1	2	3	4	5	6	7	8	9	10
11	12	13	14	15	16	17	18	19	20
21	22	23	24	25	26	27	28	29	30
31	32	33	34	35	36	37	38	39	40
41	42	43	44	45	46	47	48	49	50
51	52	53	54	55	56	57	58	59	60
61	62	63	64	65	66	67	68	69	70
71	72	73	74	75	76	77	78	79	80
81	82	83	84	85	86	87	88	89	90
91	92	93	94	95	96	97	98	99	100

Apex Maths 6 © Cambridge University Press 2003

Multiplication square

x	1	2	3	4	5	6	7	8	9	10
1	1	2	3	4	5	6	7	8	9	10
2	2	4	6	8	10	12	14	16	18	20
3	3	6	9	12	15	18	21	24	27	30
4	4	8	12	16	20	24	28	32	36	40
5	5	10	15	20	25	30	35	40	45	50
6	6	12	18	24	30	36	42	48	54	60
7	7	14	21	28	35	42	49	56	63	70
8	8	16	24	32	40	48	56	64	72	80
9	9	18	27	36	45	54	63	72	81	90
10	10	20	30	40	50	60	70	80	90	100

Apex Maths 6 © Cambridge University Press 2003

Big time 1

60 minutes make an hour.

a What time is it 100 minutes after the start of this year?

b At what time . . . of what day . . . of what month is it 100 days after the start of this year?

Big time 2

At what time . . . of what day . . . of what month . . . of what year is it

a 2000 seconds after the start of this year?

b 2000 minutes after the start of this year?

Big time 3

At what time . . . of what day . . . of what month . . . of what year is it

a 5000 hours after the start of this year?

b 5000 days after the start of this year?

Bargain trainers 1

The Super Sports shop is holding a sale of Zoom trainers for one week.

The full price of Zoom trainers is £100.

Monday: Zoom trainers reduced by 20%!

Tuesday: 25% discount on yesterday's price!

Wednesday: 50% discount on Tuesday's price!

Thursday: Reduction of 10% on Wednesday's price!

Friday: A further £2 off Zoom trainers!

What is the price of Zoom trainers on Friday?

Apex Maths 6   © Cambridge University Press 2003

Bargain trainers 2

The Super Sports shop is holding a sale of Zoom trainers for one week.

Monday: Zoom trainers reduced by 20%!

Tuesday: 25% discount on yesterday's price!

Wednesday: 50% discount on Tuesday's price!

Thursday: Reduction of 10% on Wednesday's price!

Friday: A further £2 off!

Saturday: 10% discount on Friday's price! Zoom trainers now only £22.50!

You buy the Zoom trainers on Saturday.

How much money do you save on the original price?

Apex Maths 6   © Cambridge University Press 2003

Grid squares

A 2 × 2 grid has five squares: four 1 × 1 squares and one 2 × 2 square.

1 A 3 × 3 grid has 14 squares.

Can you find them all?

a How many 1 × 1 squares? _____   **b** How many 2 × 2 squares? _____

c How many 3 × 3 squares? _____

2 Complete this table.

grid size	number of					total
	1 × 1 squares	2 × 2 squares	3 × 3 squares	4 × 4 squares	5 × 5 squares	
1 × 1	1	0	0	0	0	1
2 × 2	4	1	0	0	0	5
3 × 3						
4 × 4						
5 × 5						

3 Describe any patterns you see in the table.

_____

_____

_____

Economical boxes 1

Freya is making a box with a hinged lid out of one piece of card.

It will hold 24 centimetre cubes.

Work out the length, breadth and height of the box that will use the least amount of card.

What area of card does it use?

Apex Maths 6   © Cambridge University Press 2003

Economical boxes 2

Toni is making an open box from card.

It will hold 48 centimetre cubes.

She uses the least amount of card possible.

How much card does she use?

Apex Maths 6   © Cambridge University Press 2003

Investigating diagonals

Magic shapes 1

4   5   6   7   8   9

Write a number in each circle.

Use each number only once.

The total of each line of three numbers must be **21**.

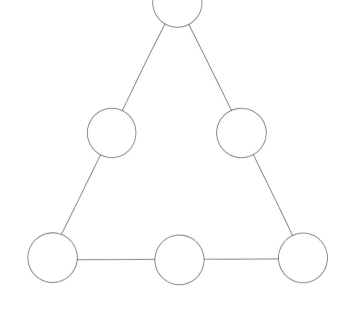

Apex Maths 6   © Cambridge University Press 2003

Name   Date

Magic shapes 2

1   2   3   4   5   6   7   8   9   10   11   12

Write a number in each circle.

Use each number only once.

Four numbers have been put in for you.

The total of each line of four numbers must be **26**.

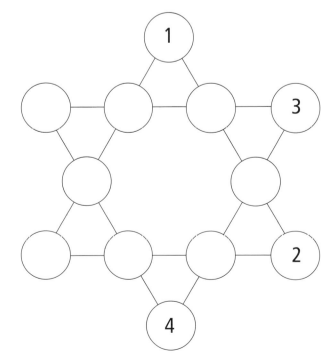

Apex Maths 6   © Cambridge University Press 2003

Magic shapes 3

21 22 23 24 25 26 27 28 29 30 31 32

Write a number in each circle.

Use each number only once.

Four numbers have been put in for you.

The total of each line of four numbers must be **106**.

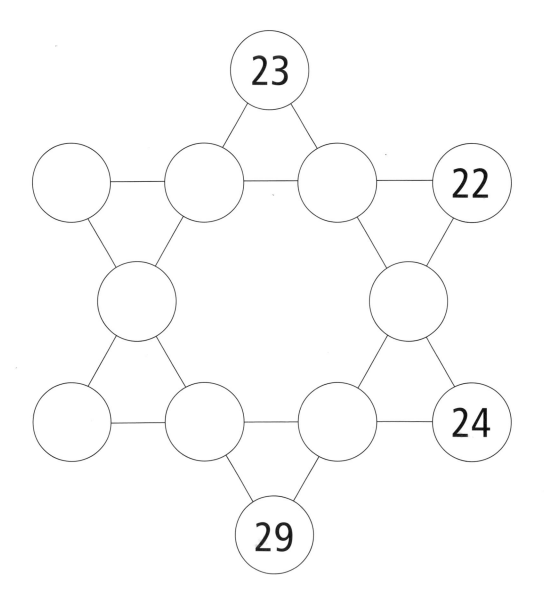